IN THE

NOBLE HILLS

*Recalling a rural American Childhood
of the 1940s and 1950s . . .*

Wes Marshall

M MORRE
BEST WISHES + ENJOY
THE MEMORIES.
WES MARSHALL
MAR 04

Printed by West Press.
Tucson, Arizona.

For

San Miguel Books
Tucson, Arizona

Cover Photograph by Wes Marshall

Copyright © 2000 [First Printing 2004]

All Rights Reserved
San Miguel Books
5550 E. Miles Circle
Tucson, AZ. 85712

Printed in the United States of America

Cataloging in Publication Data

Wesley B. Marshall
Noble Hills: A Memoir

ISBN: 0-9747584-0-X

Library of Congress Control Number 2003099070

FOR

My wife, Marilyn

My parents, Bae and Mary Marshall

*And for all those who share memories
of living in Noble County, Ohio*

The author will donate one-quarter of all book sales revenue to the Noble County Historical Society

NOBLE HILLS

A Sense of Place 1

PART I: REMEMBERING

PART II: GOING BACK

A SENSE OF PLACE

This book recalls events and people that touched my life as a young boy. The stories are a combination of fact and fiction. What could not be clearly remembered was recreated with a narrative more focused on ambiance and characterization than on historic accuracy. This book, therefore, is not so much an account of Noble County or Caldwell village history as it is a recollection of life in a rural Southeastern Ohio community during and following World War II.

It is now an easy thirty-minute drive from the village of Caldwell south down Interstate 77 to Marietta, Ohio and the confluence of the Ohio and Muskingum Rivers, but when I was growing up in Noble County in the 1940s and 50s, an automobile trip to the river took at least an hour. US Route 21 was a crooked, two-lane highway that wandered through the small hamlets of Dexter City, Macksburg, Lower Salem and Whipple before joining

Route 7 just west of Marietta. Chunks of that old road still exist in the 21st Century.

Southern Ohio counties, including Noble, are at the western edge of the Allegheny Plateau. The land is hilly, heavily forested and cut with small streams. Before World War II the area was dotted with modest farms, quaint white churches and meandering cornfields. Not much has changed over the years. Now, the farms are more likely to be an avocation than a vocation, and the little white churches, though hidden from the interstate, are still there.

Noble is the smallest and youngest of Ohio's eighty-eight counties. It was formed March 11, 1851 and named after James Noble, one of the area's first settlers. The county was literally carved out of Monroe, Washington, Morgan and Guernsey counties. If Washington County were not to its south, Noble would be directly across the Ohio River from West Virginia.

The county's four hundred and four square miles surround the village of Caldwell. It is an area where old barns still sport Mail Pouch chewing tobacco signs, and antique covered bridges continue to carry traffic. On early summer mornings, a fluffy gray mist often drifts through the lowlands and around tree-covered hillsides. Along small waterways, green and yellow crops contrast with freshly plowed fields to create patchworks of bright ground color.

Historically, Noble County residents share a lifestyle similar to their Appalachian neighbors across the Ohio
River and those in Kentucky and Tennessee. Before World
War II, most of the county's twelve thousand or so
residents had something to do with farming or the business
of a county seat. Rural commerce and social activities took
place in picturesque little hamlets tucked in narrow valleys
or perched along high ridges. Most of the small villages
had a meeting hall and at least one church facing a narrow
blacktop or gravel road, and one would find a combination
gasoline station, country store and US Post Office standing
in the center of a few homes.

Following World War II, travel, an expanding
economy and mass-media chipped away at rural isolation.
Some young men returned to farming following the war,
but most looked for other opportunities. Agriculture, as a
major local economy, gave way to industry and small
businesses, and in the 1950s life cranked up a notch and
bypassed some of the simplicities of a rural American
lifestyle.

Deep shaft coal mining drove the region's economy
in earlier years, but over time strip mining replaced
underground operations. Immense machines literally
scalped the land uncovering and removing coal deposits.
Only in recent years has reforestation mended Southeastern
Ohio's mining scars. Entering the 21st Century, the

county's economy keys to tourism, interstate travel, modest manufacturing and a newly built state prison.

Before there were interstate highways, U.S. Route 21 was a major north–south throughway. Starting in Cleveland, the two-lane route passed through Caldwell on its way down into the Carolinas. Today, the four lanes of Interstate 77 replace much of that old highway, and road traffic thunders by the little village. Occasionally, travelers pull off at exit twenty-five for a bite to eat or an overnight stop in Caldwell. The exit merges with Ohio Route 78, a rural highway that ambles through the county from east to west, dividing it from north to south.

In earlier days, tourists stopped at small towns to visit historic points all along Route 21. The communities and sites are still there, but most travelers prefer the four lane superhighway and no longer pause in villages like Ava where a monument commemorates the 1925 crash of the Navy dirigible, USS Shenandoah. Close by, Captain Zachary Landowne and thirteen of his crew died in that early airship disaster. Farther south, a Johnny Appleseed monument stands along the highway. It is near what was a legendary old family roadside restaurant. Ogle's fried chicken, lemonade and homemade pies pleased many a traveler. The building is still there, but the restaurant is long gone.

This near idyllic setting was my home from the late 1930s to the late 1950s. Our family moved from New York

City to Noble County in the mid-1930s. My father had worked on Wall Street, and our relocation was prompted by the economic aftermath of the great depression. We joined my mother's family in Caldwell to run a general store. At the time, the village population was about fifteen hundred and my high school class numbered a bit over thirty.

Caldwell, Ohio in the 1950s

Intersection of Main [Vertical] & West Streets

Samuel Caldwell

". . . early pioneer settler after whom the village of Caldwell was named and who gave the ground on which the Noble County Courthouse is built . . . "

Caldwell Municipal Building Dedication Brochure
The Journal & Noble County Leader, July, 1957

Part I: Remembering

THE VILLAGE AND I

Caldwell was born at a County Commissioners meeting on December 6, 1854. Two motions were passed at that gathering. The first placed the county seat of Noble in Olive Township and designated land for streets and lots including two and a half acres for a public square. The second motion named the village in honor of Samuel Caldwell.

I was born November 4, 1934 in Brooklyn, New York, the son of Wesley B and Mary Louise Marshall. My birth certificate identifies me as Wesley Baehill Marshall, the middle name a combination of my father's middle name, Bae, and my mother's maiden name, Hill. Our home in Caldwell was an apartment on the top floor of Hill's General Store on Main Street, a short half block east of the village square.

Regardless of the name on my birth certificate, I was known as "Skibo" through most of my early childhood. The nickname probably came from a connection between my mother's college days at Carnegie Technological University and a Scottish castle named Skibo, (once owned by Andrew Carnegie), but I will never know for sure. Anyway, the name stuck well into high school.

My earliest village memories come from the almost daily walks my mother and I made to Woody's meat market. We would stroll up Main Street to where the Noble County Courthouse sat in the midst of large shade trees, beige cement sidewalks and small flower gardens. Passing a drug store on the corner, our journey would take us across Cumberland Street, through a cluster of green park benches on the east esplanade of the square and then northwest toward the Farmers and Merchants Bank.

In the summer, the sweet scent of fresh cut grass filled the air. In the fall, piles of red and golden leaves littered the ground, just right for jumping into or scattering to the winds. In the winter, footprints meandered here and there in new snow, and rock salt covered sidewalks that bordered and crisscrossed the area. Traffic lights on each of the square's four corners helped control the movement of pedestrians, automobiles, trucks and horse-drawn wagons.

U.S. Route 21 entered Caldwell from the northwest, ambled south on Miller and then east down a tree lined North Street where it humped up over the old Pennsylvania railroad viaduct before turning south again to form one side of the square. I loved to watch big trucks try to make the turn at the corner of North and West streets in front of Ralston's Drug Store without running over the curb or hitting a street sign. Many did both.

Our trips to the market frequently involved a detour through the courthouse because nature called; at least that is what my mother presumed. As a youngster, I was fascinated with the large white marble urinals neatly spaced along one wall of the tiled Men's room, each with its shiny chrome handle. I would do my thing in the furthest cubicle and then flush all of them on my way out. Back then, the facilities were not cleaned as frequently, or as well, as they might have been. The pervasive odor was one of overflowing brass spittoons mixed with the essence of what was referred to in our family as *number one*.

The walk took us by McVay's furniture store as we headed up North Street. The folks who owned the store also operated one of the village's funeral homes. Woody's meat market was a smallish place with a big cold storage locker. Sawdust covered the floor and sticky flypaper dangled from the tin ceiling. Woody was a short ruddy chap who wore a stained white bib apron, was mostly cheerful and nearly always greeted me with a friendly, "Hi, Skibo."

The meat counter was about as high as I was tall so my view was eye-level. Fascinated, I would watch Woody swing a heavy cleaver, chopping away at big chunks of red meat. It never occurred to me one could lose fingers doing that. My cousin, Tally, remembers getting free hot dogs at the store. She now characterizes the treat as being, "Safe to eat raw back at the time." Whatever my mother bought was wrapped in brown paper and carried home to cook that very night because our ice box was not cold enough to safely keep meat or poultry for any length of time.

I was six years old when I walked into Miss Pearl Newton's first grade classroom. The elementary school buildings were on the south side of North Street perched on a hill just east of the railroad tracks. Long steep steps climbed up to the crest of the hill from both the north and south. A playground, mostly topped with cinders and some trees, surrounded the brick buildings. The harsh ground cover contributed to scraped elbows and pants with shredded knees.

The oldest school building housed grades four through six. Both structures had outside iron fire escapes that reached up to a second floor and were regularly used during drills. We all sat at small fixed wooden desks with blackened inkwells and battered tops. Countless initials scarred the varnished wood surface. Black chalkboards circled most of the classroom, the writing surface painted with white horizontal lines to guide printing upper and lowercase letters. On either side of the building entrance, dark red bricks and young children were daily powdered white with chalk dust from cleaning blackboard erasers.

Getting to grade school involved crossing the square, hiking up North Street, going by the Presbyterian Church and then the home of my aunt and uncle, Bill and Kathleen Hill. The boys' common attire in 1942 was knickers (with suspenders), long socks, ankle high shoes and an itchy wool sweater. Girls wore dresses and long socks, and nearly everyone had big black four-buckle galoshes for the winter snows.

Early on, my roaming territory was defined by sound. When my mother wanted me, she would stand on our upstairs front porch and yell, "S-k-i-b-o." If my response was slow, I was in trouble.

The auditory boundary was later expanded by telephone. My mother would call the local operator and ask her to locate me. It was not unusual, therefore, for someone at a drug store, filling station or friend's home to tell me Mother had called and I was to go home.

Using the phone as a *person finder* was not limited to me or to locating children. Many of us routinely asked the operator to track down one or both parents. Party lines were common, and phones only came in one color and type, black with no dial. We all knew the operators by first name, and phone numbers were easy to remember. Our home phone was 207-M and the store was simply 31. I have often wondered if the numbers were assigned in the order in which telephones were installed.

My awareness of the village and surrounding area expanded with the arrival of a red American Flyer bicycle one Christmas morning. It sported lots of chrome, fat tires, rigid fenders, a front light and a little bell. While peddling around and beyond Caldwell, any thought that the village was quaint or picturesque never entered my mind, but I was aware of the brick streets because they were uneven and rough on a bike. I saw, but did not think about, two-story white houses sitting well back in deep shady lawns. Many homes had a garden, a cast iron pump to pull water from a well or cistern and a small wooden outhouse.

Riding about, my buddies and I learned the village was truly tucked into gently rolling hills. Two major east–west streets ran from the high west-end down to a low valley on the east. Caldwell was almost totally encircled by Duck Creek, a meandering, murky brown stream that eventually emptied into the Ohio River and tended to flood each spring. Entering or leaving Caldwell, in all but one direction, required crossing a bridge. Many times we swam under the silver iron structure that spanned the creek on Route 285 going out to Sarahsville.

The bikes gave us freedom to explore in and out of the village. A lumberyard on the edge of town had a large sand pile we could not resist. Playing in the dark moist sand, we could hear large mill saws whine, loudly creating fragrant piles of sawdust. And there was a building the county used to store rock salt for winter streets.

Fortunately, none of us were injured or suffocated playing and tunneling in mounds of the caustic crumbling crystals.

We often rode down along the Pennsylvania Railroad tracks to the underside of the North Street viaduct where a short climb up the bridge's vertical abutment provided access to a narrow opening that led into a dim scary cavern. There was no good reason to be in that stinky place except the adventure of doing so. Nearby, stacks of lumber piled along the railroad track provided something to climb on and a near perfect venue for hide-and-seek

Those early childhood memories are filled with thoughts of warm fresh bakery goods, sacks of nails from the hardware, cap pistols from the five and dime, nickel-a-scoop ice cream cones, Saturday afternoon matinees starring Gene Autry and a traditional family treat of Sunday supper dessert. Following dinner, it was my job to walk up to a nearby restaurant for a pint of hand-packed vanilla ice cream and a bag of Planter's Peanuts. The ice cream and nuts got topped with dark rich chocolate syrup from a Hershey can that, no matter what you did with it, always remained sticky.

Village merchants sold everything from food to insurance. There were men's all-wool suits, bib overalls and white shirts with detachable stiff collars and women's gingham dresses. Grocery markets offered fresh fruit from open baskets and summer corn stacked out front next to piles of melons. There was a blacksmith shop near us and an implement company that sold hemp rope and green and yellow John Deer tractors.

Hill's Store was across Main Street from the Permian Oil and Gas Company. A true general store, it sold everything from cheese to shoes to wallpaper. The basic building was two and a half stories high and constructed of extremely hard, hand-formed concrete block.

Just down the street from the store, farmers deposited big stainless steel cans of milk each weekday morning to be processed into bottles for hand delivery. Across the street, Murphy's offered a variety of furniture and, like McVay's, provided funeral services. One block beyond the creamery, Main Street ended at a cow pasture we called Ball's field.

Years later, as an adult reflecting back on early childhood, I would remember the village well. Those memories would be of a time when religious and political beliefs were typically conservative. Family units were functional and important to everyday life. Aging parents lived with their adult children and young grandchildren because there were no retirement homes as we know them today. Basically, family looked after family, neighbor after neighbor and friend after friend.

Back then crime was largely petty. There were minor robberies and some folks got caught making whiskey but not much more. Life was simple, generally predictable and uncomplicated until a Sunday in December changed the world. I do remember Pearl Harbor, but as a child, I had no clear sense of what it meant. War was an adult thing. For those of us growing up in the early 1940s, it was just something to play along with Cowboy and Indians. Only years later would I understand the terrible consequence many families experienced through the loss of loved ones.

If there was poverty in Caldwell and Noble County when I grew up, I did not see it. If there were minorities, I did not recognize them as a child. If there was violence, it did not touch me. There was war rationing, a shortage of gasoline and no new tires, but I was never hungry, bored or denied anything I really needed.

It seems likely most folks consider their early childhood unique. Yet, for those of us who lived and grew up in rural America at that time, life was special. We played and learned, loved and laughed, pouted and cried and grew up in a gentle safe place. Only much later would our world become a more violent one threatened by nuclear holocaust and economically challenged by multinational greed.

Our life was a simple one where planning for the future did not go much beyond the next day or week. The little village was our home and, years later, a place to revisit. Now, for some of us, the visual and emotional memories of life back then are forever fixed in our minds.

Many of us moved from that wonderful, caring place, but it will forever remain deep within our hearts.

USS AVENGER

J.R. and I were good buddies; our families lived in upstairs apartments across Main Street from each other. Second floor living was unusual in our rural Ohio village so we thought we were pretty special. It was easy to use our Captain America secret decoder rings to signal back and fourth from his balcony to my porch. We had the deluxe models with miniature sundials that glowed in the dark.

On a sunny late spring morning in 1944, we were hanging out on the steps of the weekly newspaper. School was out and we looked forward to a summer of freedom. I was ten and J.R. was some younger. The clickety-clack of a Linotype came from a nearby window, the sound drifting along with the smell of hot lead.

It was our second day of discussing a big building project. The previous weekend we had seen newsreels of US Navy PT boats fighting in the Pacific. The spirit of World War II was strong in our little town. Many of us had, or knew, fathers and brothers who were off to the war.

So it seemed right for us to build the first PT boat ever to float on Duck Creek, or as it was locally called, "The Crick."

Having never seen a real PT boat, or for that matter any Navy ship, neither of us had any sense of scale. But we figured a battleship would take too long to build and more lumber than we could get. My family was part owner of the general store I lived above. It sold linoleum in ten and twelve-foot rolls packaged and shipped in wooden crates. For reasons that never made sense to me, the floor covering was displayed on the building's top floor.

There was a big old lift system up there with geared wheels, ropes and pulleys. Using it, the crates were hoisted up to the display area and, in exchange for cranking the system and taking the crates apart, I could keep the lumber. This wood was used to build a rambling tree house, roofing for a secret tunnel, Army vehicles and more.

I had a hammer and J.R. had a saw. Between the two of us we had twenty-three cents for building costs. A dime bought more nails than one could easily carry. Generally, bigger was better because the wood was hard, and we bent more nails than we pounded straight. But, the real challenge was to get our money past the bakery on the way to the hardware. Ten cents would also buy two really big peanut butter cookies fresh out of the oven.

By mid-morning, we had two crates apart and about sixteen long boards piled in a shed attached to the

store. That done, J.R. and I headed to the hardware store.
It had an oiled wood floor and wonderful items piled to the
ceiling. The high oak ladder was fun to ride along a
wheeled track on one side of the store. The clerk let us go
behind the counter to select and rake the nails out of
wooden bins into brown paper sacks. We gave him our
dime and headed home with black smudgy hands. Our
supplies now included several pounds of nails and two
peanut butter cookies, having not made it by the bakery on
the way back.

The PT boat in the newsreel had a nice pointed
bow, but we had no idea how to do that. So, our ship
would have a square front and back and torpedo tubes on
each side. Sawing away on the lumber, we talked about
what to call our boat. The sneak attack on Pearl Harbor
was a strong image in our young minds and from that
memory evolved the name, USS Avenger.

The boat's design was influenced by our realization
that somehow we had to get it down to the creek. That
would involve lugging it a block or so to the east-end of
Main Street and up over a barbed wire fence into Mr. Ball's
cow pasture. From there it was maybe a hundred yards to a
sloped spot on the bank. Our thinking was that we could
get a six-foot long by three-foot wide boat onto J.R.'s
battered red Radio Flyer wagon.

With the bottom and sides of our ship in place, the
second day started with a hunt for paint and something to

make the boat waterproof. J.R. lived above a natural gas company office and garage. Out behind his building we found an old piece of rusted tin big enough to cover the bottom of our boat and then some. We also found a large can of what appeared to be thick red paint. We pounded the tin around the bottom, nailed it in place and were delighted to see the metal reach part way up the sides, front and back. Cardboard centers from a linoleum roll became the torpedo tubes. With that done, it was time to paint. The red stuff was hard to spread, but we managed to coat the outside and most of the inside of our boat.

Three days later the paint was still tacky. It would be messy, but we could not wait any longer to get Avenger into the water. With a big effort, we humped it up onto the wagon and headed down Main Street. I pulled with a rope and J.R. pushed. We clattered along to the amusement of neighborhood adults and the dismay of drivers. The day before we had found an empty Heinz ketchup bottle we could use to christen our ship. Its residue matched the red paint smeared on both of us. Getting the heavy mass over the fence was a task that resulted in numerous scratches over most of our bodies. But you couldn't much tell the blood from the paint or the ketchup.

With the boat on it, the wagon wheels quickly sank into the damp field and refused to move. We heaved the boat off the wagon and, with both of us pulling, managed to slide the bulk along the ground, leaving a trail of flat red-stained grass. Tuckered out by our effort, we rested and drank sweet colored liquid from a stash of little hollow wax bottles. When the drink was gone, one could chew the wax into something resembling gum.

High on sugar and growing anticipation, we got back to our task. Following an appropriate little speech by me, J.R. swung the ketchup bottle down onto the bow. The glass did not break, but it put a big-time dent in the wood. Two more swings had the same result so we skipped the christening and went to the launching. The slope of the bank was about forty-five degrees. We tipped the bow over the edge and shoved. USS Avenger slid silently down six feet of dirt into the water. It did not pause one second before sinking out of sight. There was not a bubble or a sound. The front of the boat just went slowly under water and the rest followed. Nothing came back up.

We were stunned! How could this be? We searched for some explanation. Doesn't wood float? How come the tin and paint didn't make it waterproof? No answers came to mind. J.R. looked at me, his expression saying, *all that work for nothing*. He and I looked again to make sure our boat hadn't surfaced on down the crick. It hadn't. Then my buddy smiled and said, "Well . . . I guess we made a submarine." His observation struck me as funny. Both of us started laughing. We ended up rolling on the grass and then watching lazy clouds drift by above. The summer of '44 was underway.

Years later, as a young reporter, I photographed the construction of a school building in a nearby town. Slowly a hazy memory formed in the back of my mind as I watched plumbers smear red sticky goop onto black iron water pipes. The stuff came from a highly stained can labeled lead pipe dope. Closing my eyes, I could visualize J.R. and me painting our PT boat years before, and then I understood one of the reasons the red stuff never dried and USS Avenger never floated.

HILL'S GENERAL STORE

For many locals, a day in Caldwell involved a stop at Hill's Store where you could buy a wide variety of goods including shoes, cotton quilt batting, slabs of Colby cheese or a gallon of paint. Compared to the Super K-Marts of the late nineteen hundreds, Hill's was inky-dinky. Yet, both businesses served the same purpose: to provide a little bit of everything for everybody. The difference was, in the early 1940s, there was not as much of everything to sell.

As a young child, the store seemed immense to me. Our top floor apartment occupied two thirds of that level. A large living room stretched across the full width of the building's front, and a narrow hallway ran down the middle of the apartment ending in a doorway to the linoleum display area. Like compartments on a railroad car, four bedrooms tracked down one side of a central hallway. A bathroom, kitchen, breakfast room and dining-family area marched down the other side of the corridor. The ceilings were high and the floor sagged significantly.

25

The main building was built of hand-formed concrete block, probably sometime in the late 1800s. It was about a quarter of a village block wide overall by a half block long. Sometime later, a shed-like addition was added to the building's east side. That space originally served as a livery stable and later as dry goods storage.

A low balcony at the rear of the building created a short second floor and housed a small office, a collection of wallpaper sample books and cans of paint. A hand-operated elevator ran from the basement to the third floor in the early years.

How the creaky old lift worked was always a mystery to me because I did not understand the physics of the system. But I quickly learned which rope to pull to slowly move it up and down. In retrospect, it must have been a well counter-balanced design for a person my size to work it at that young age.

The store's main floor was made of dark creaky wood. I would sometimes be paid a few cents to spread, and then sweep up, green gritty looking stuff along with the dust and debris. The cleaner left a pungent, but not unpleasant smell. Daylight coming through large front windows facing south onto Main Street caused the treated floor to shine. The front door was flanked by window display areas that always featured merchandise of some sort. Out front, above a big canvas awning, a large red and green neon sign spelled *Hill's.*

Counters lined both outside walls and ran down the center of the main floor forming two aisles. The low second floor balcony, office and stairway were visible to anyone entering the front door. It was common to see my father sitting in the small glass-enclosed work area smoking his pipe, doing books, designing a floor covering layout or chatting on the phone.

In the early years, a modest grocery section occupied the area under the balcony at the very rear of the store. There were more brands of cigarettes than dry cereal. Cookies came in open boxes and soda crackers were sold from wooden barrels. Baskets of fruit and dried beans were stacked about. Big red slabs of bologna hung from the low ceiling over a countertop where large rounds of Colby cheese sat casually covered with cheesecloth. The aroma of freshly ground coffee beans spilled from a large electric grinder used by many customers. Lunch for me was often a slice of meat and a cut of cheese in between soda crackers that were, by contemporary packaging standards, quite stale.

The first fish I recall seeing, other than from a stream or lake, were in a barrel of salt brine. Silver scales glistening, they lay stacked in layers, staring up at me with gaping mouths and glassy eyes just smelling awful. Surely, I thought, no one would eat fish like that, but people did. It would be many years before I elected to eat any seafood and, to this day, the choice excludes anything with eyes.

The basement stairs were under the balcony access. Going down there was like descending into a dungeon, because it was a mysterious damp place that I truly believed housed demons, zombies and wicked witches. Never did I see or encounter such creatures, but you could not convince me they were not there just waiting to pounce on me and my buddies.

The large coal-fired furnace marginally heated the store. It was my father's nightly winter task to stoke the furnace and make sure there was sufficient coal in it to last the night. It was a mechanical marvel to me, and I never tired of watching him pull and shake a big lever that mechanically dumped hot coals down into a glowing red ash pile. Periodically, someone delivered coal, shoveling it from a truck through a small window and down a short wooden trough into a basement storage bin. On those days, coal dust just went everywhere and got onto everything, including us kids.

The leftover ash and cinders had to be shoveled back out the same little basement window and often spread on sidewalks in the winter to cover snow and ice. Then the residue was tracked back into the store on wet boots. Somehow the entire process seemed like a lot of effort for a system that never generated enough heat to reach our apartment. What little living area warmth we had came from open natural gas heaters. Sleeping rooms were unheated and it was not unusual to encounter ice on the *inside* of the window on a cold winter morning.

As a child, I spent a good deal of time in the store. Bulk candy was easily available and lots of our family friends shopped there. Every week or so, Mr. Paisley would arrive with suitcases full of samples. He was more than a traveling salesman. To my father and uncles, he was a source of information and jokes. He always had new products to offer and he knew how business was going in other communities.

But for me, the truly special treat was sitting in his brand new automobile and pretending I was driving. He always had the latest and biggest cars, usually Buicks. We owned an old Willys coupe with a rumble seat and it was neat, but Mr. Paisley's shiny new black Buick had nearly as much chrome as it did paint. It was a momentous occasion the first time he drove up with an automatic transmission and no clutch.

Store clerks were long-time local residents and mostly ladies. The interaction between customers and salespersons was more like a friendly visit than a sales event. Everyone knew everyone one else. There was no pressure to buy anything. Questions were answered if asked. There were no dressing rooms. Folks just wandered around gathering items and, when finished, they would deposit everything at a central counter to have the bill written up. Transactions were almost always in cash.

Everything, from clothing to yard goods and sweets, was displayed in the open and accessible for examination or to be sampled, especially candy and cookies. Colorful thread and yarn centers brightened part of one area. Green glass dividers, two or three inches high, fastened together with metal clips, separated countertop items. The old mechanical cash register clanked away, never failing to work. One counter top had a yardstick tacked to an edge for measuring fabric and lace. The window blind display was a particular fascination for me. Trimming and cutting blinds to size required a variety of neat tools that I often borrowed and was yelled at for not returning.

Daily life at the store included smells not so common in later years. Kerosene was sold in bulk and hand pumped into tin storage containers for use in glass lanterns. Packages of Mail Pouch, Redman and other chewing tobacco brands emitted a strong pungent odor. Ball Band rubber boots smelled like new tires. Cigarette and pipe smoke was everywhere. Air conditioning and deodorant were yet to come, perfume was overused and the smell of perspiration on a hot summer day was quite normal.

The closest thing to a playground I had was the big canvas awning out front. It spanned the width of the store and could be rolled up and down with a long handled crank. When it was down, four iron pipes folded out horizontally to support the structure. The pipes were irresistible. One could swing, chin and *skin the cat* when sidewalk traffic was light. More than once, I crashed to the concrete with bruised and woozy results.

I am not sure, but I suspect nearly all Caldwell businesses were locally owned and operated. In truth, the community leadership rested with the merchants. My father was a member, and then President, of the Caldwell Exempted Village School Board. Others served on the Village Council, Chamber of Commerce or with the Volunteer Fire Department. Unlike large chain retailers of later years, there were no stockholders demanding high investment profits. Most businesses provided a good living for the owners and workers.

Many years would pass before I began to understand the true nature of merchandising back then. On the rare occasion a product did not meet an acceptable standard, it was returned or exchanged with no questions asked. Sometimes there was not enough money to pay for basic essentials so folks ran an account, and it was rare for anyone to receive a letter demanding payment. People would pay what they could each month, and occasionally a debt would be reduced in trade for produce or service.

I returned to Caldwell in the fall of 1970 for my father's funeral. Hill's Store had changed hands by then; indeed it may have been closed. The food section was the first to go when chain grocery stores opened on and off the square. Drugstores became the source for tobacco products and candy. Clothing stores started to sell overalls and shoes along with wool suits. Hardware stores added paint and wallpaper. The product erosion continued until there wasn't much left to sell at Hill's. So, in our little village and elsewhere in America, the true general store faded away only to return generations later as Wal-Mart.

The *viewing* as it was called, took place the night before the funeral. Friends and folks were invited to pay their respects to the family and observe the deceased for the last time. As an only child, whose mother had died earlier, I stood there alone greeting what seemed to be an endless line of people. Some I knew, but many were complete strangers. Why, I wondered, did so many folks take the time to stop?

My depression worsened as the evening progressed, making it hard to be pleasant and responsive. As the line neared its end, an elderly couple shuffled forward, their dress suggesting they were farmers and not from the village. Both expressed their condolences and turned to leave. The old man's face was deeply tanned except for a white forehead that had been forever shaded by the battered straw hat he clutched in a trembling hand. Then they both paused and turned back to me. The women held a damp white lace handkerchief. The man struggled to find the right words, moisture glinting in the corner of his eyes.

"You probably don't know us," he said. "We're from up near Fulda now, you know. The old farm ain't much anymore. But back when your father and uncles was with the store, they all helped us when we didn't have no money. We both come here tonight to pay our respects and to say thanks." They shook my hand as they departed, and from then on, my sense of life's values changed forever.

Hill's General Store Building (1999)

FREE ENTERPRISE

C.C. slowly ambled up the street toward me, August heat shimmering off his twelve-year old body. Sighing loudly, he joined me on the curb across the street from Hill's Store. We sat there silently watching cars and people mosey up and down Main Street.

"What-cha doing?" I asked.

"Ain't doing nothin," C.C. replied.

"Me neither." (Long pause) "You wanna go down to the crick and shoot some?"

"Ain't got no BBs."

"Me neither." (Longer pause) "You got any money?"

"Naw."

"Me neither. What would you do if you had some?"

"Money?"

"Yea . . . maybe even a dollar."

"Well, I'd go right up to Ralston's and get me a big old soda with double chocolate."

The image of a big old soda formed in my mind. I visualized a nice tall glass with beads of moisture and drips of chocolate spilling down the sides. I could see a candy striped straw poking up out of a glob of pure white whipped cream and I could almost taste the rich dark chocolate, fizzy bubbles and vanilla ice cream. It was nearly more than a totally broke eleven-year old could stand.

C.C. picked up a pebble and flipped it at a nearby electric pole. The stone hit the wood with a subtle thunk and dropped to the street. "What-cha thinking?"

"I'm thinking we got to get us some money. Maybe we could mow Grandma Croy's yard again; she's good for a quarter a piece."

"Naw, we just did that a few days ago."

"How about we make some lemonade and sell it over by the store?"

C.C. glanced hard at me, disbelief clear in his expression. "We ain't got no ice and no one's gonna buy warm lemonade on a day like this."

The minutes passed in silence, our minds slipping into neutral until something I was watching fully registered. Across the street, shoppers were going into Hill's store and coming out with brown paper bags full of stuff. An idea began to form. "You know, C.C., maybe there's a way we could make some money."

"How's that?"

"You see all those sacks people are carrying out over there?"

"Yea. So what?"

"Well, suppose we sold em' sacks when they went *into* the store."

C.C. looked at me, over at the store and then back. "Where'd we get sacks?"

"They're back in the warehouse in big piles."

"You could just take some?"

C.C.'s "take some," sounded like stealing, and that wasn't exactly what I had in mind. "Well, maybe we could sort of *borrow* some."

"O.K., we borrow some, then what?"

"We'd be out in front and catch people on the way in. That way they'd have their own sack."

"You sure that'd work?"

"Let's see," I answered and started across the street.

C.C. followed me down the alley along the side of the store and around back to a big sliding door that was supposed to be locked but rarely was. It opened quietly, and we slipped into a nearly dark storage area. Back under a shallow loft we found the paper bags, neatly bundled and stacked on a shelf ready to use. C.C. and I grabbed a handful and slipped back outside. Before moving around to the front of the store, we made a small, cardboard sign that read:

Sacks for Sale
1¢.

The steps going up into the store were flanked by two small cavities built to let light into low basement windows. We got down into one of the shallow wells. The space was big enough for us to sit in and almost always full of wind-blown trash. It wasn't long before customers saw our sign and, mostly in amusement, stopped to buy a brown paper sack. In a little over an hour, we were sold out and thinking about two chocolate sodas when my father came down the steps, stopped, and stood in front of us. He was a tall slight man with combed back dark hair and an angular face that usually sported a smile. When it did not, I had learned to be cautious.

"How are you boys doing?" He asked.

"We're doing okay." I answered.

C.C. opted to remain quiet.

"How much money did you make?"

"Ah, we sold fifty-three sacks."

"Well, that's pretty good."

C.C. nodded.

"And where did you get the sacks?" He asked, looking directly at me.

"Oh, well . . . we sort of borrowed them."

"You mean you took them on consignment."

C.C. and I glanced at each other, both thinking the conversation wasn't going in a positive direction. "I don't know what you mean."

Smiling just slightly, my father answered. "Sometimes in business you get merchandise to sell without paying for it up front. Then, when you do sell it, you pay for it. That's called getting something on consignment."

"Uh-huh. I guess that's what we did."

Pausing to greet customers entering the store, my father then sat down on the lowest step and continued. "Now let's see son, you sold fifty-three sacks at a penny a piece?"

"Yep," I said as C.C. bobbed his head in agreement.

"Okay, you owe the store fifty-three cents for the merchandise."

Our images of chocolate sodas faded. "But that's all we made."

"Yes, but that's not the store's fault. If you'd checked before you started and found out the sacks were a penny a piece, you could have sold them for two cents and made a profit."

Beginning to suspect this was an adult line of reasoning against which there was no youthful argument, I made one last appeal. "You don't charge for the sacks."

"That's right, we don't sell sacks. People who buy merchandise get them free, but we still have to buy them."

C.C. and I just looked at him, trying our best to appear sad as I handed over the fifty-three cents.

My father took the pennies and looked thoughtfully at the two of us before speaking. "I have a proposition for you. Suppose I sold you sacks for a penny each and you, in turn, sold them to customers for two cents. Would you like to go into business?"

A smile worked its way onto our young faces. C.C. answered. "Sure, we'd make a penny a sack?"

"Yes, and you'd get a couple of dollars a day."

Wow, we thought, what a great idea. "When do we start?"

Looking serious, my father continued. "Tomorrow morning at eight and you get a half hour off for lunch and we close at five, six days a week"

The total horror of his explanation must have instantly registered on our faces because he then laughed and said, "Of course its summer, schools' out, and you're not supposed to be working all the time."

C.C. and I looked a little less grim.

Standing and reaching into his pocket, he removed two bright shiny quarters and gave one to each of us. Then, pointing to the trash in the window wells, he said, "Clean that up and then go have a soda on me."

LITTLE PONDS & SILVER BRIDGES

"Trim the mainsail and hoist the battle flags," the Captain shouted. "Turn her into the wind, Mr. Quigley, and roll out the guns." Old Ironsides slowly, majestically came about, her battle ensigns flying. As she settled into a new course, smoke and fire erupted from her sides sending hot cannon balls into the British frigate. "Show no mercy, me lads," the Captain called, waving his cutlass in the moist air, casting a mystical spell on all. But, the spell broke when three cows wandered over to see what was going on.

What they saw was a ten-year-old boy standing up to his knees in a shallow pond in the middle of Mr. Ball's field. Born in the spring rains, only to disappear in the dog days of August, the little body of water was home to a host of small flying insects, darting tadpoles and a fleet of great sailing ships.

Made from orange crate wood, wrapping twine and bits of old family sheets, the little craft sailed over the shallow water or were urged along with guide strings.

Round pebbles served as cannon balls, and stacks of rocks became pirate forts. Youthful creative thinking generated unending battle scenarios that consumed hours of summer time and amused the cows, if they had a sense of humor.

Imagination was the key to a boredom-free life for an only child in a small rural village. A pearl handled cap pistol was enough to transform a gangly young boy into a handsome cowboy riding off into a purple sunset on his faithful white horse. An old grain sack, tied around the neck, was just right to become Superman – or Super-woman. And, with a tiny bit of fantasy, a murky little pond easily became a great ocean and the stage for historic sea battles.

But mostly, kids played with other kids. There were probably days when we sat around wondering what to do, but I don't remember them. In various iterations, the east-side gang consisted of three boys and four girls. There was no real boy-girl awareness, except some of us had dolls and some had footballs. But thanks to our imaginations, we could be whatever we dreamed to be.

A lot of our play took place around Mrs. Croy's big, two-story white house down at the end of Main Street. In spirit at least, she was a grandmother to all of us. It was cool that she had a water pump right in her kitchen next to the sink and not far from a cookie jar always full of homemade goodies. Her big front yard trees provided places for hide and seek, and the large grassy lawn was chameleon-like. One moment it was a football field, the next minute a western prairie with screaming Indians and then a battlefield with Axis enemies. In a summer downpour, the wet grass was something to slide on and, in the winter, mounds of snow became forts from which snowballs constantly erupted to the dismay of the unwary passersby.

Grandma Croy had a wonderful old dusty-musty shed and a creaky two-car garage. The garage was full of cardboard boxes overflowing with yellow National Geographic and Life magazines and other moldy stuff. A rambling front porch wrapped around two sides of her house and featured several cushioned gliders and an assortment of rocking chairs. Apple trees grew along one edge of her property and, picked green, never failed to give us an early spring stomachache.

For young, creative minds, small wheels in nearly any form were a precious commodity. With them, one could create tanks, racing cars, airplanes and scooters. Baby carriage wheels were especially neat. They were light and had rubber tires and wire spokes. I suspect mothers hid their carriages during the day to protect them from the east-end scavengers. Our vehicular creations were all powered by kids or gravity. Endless hours were spent pushing each other along sidewalks or screaming down hilly back streets. Steering mechanisms were primitive and crashes were frequent. Fortunately, no one ever got hit by a car or had anything more serious than skinned elbows and knees.

The tree house down along the cow pasture fence line was an architectural and structural marvel, in our view. Or, for adults, it was probably considered a major winter eyesore when tree limbs were bare. It precariously rambled out along several branches over multiple levels and featured a rusted tin roof above a "secret" trap door known to all. The color scheme was eclectic, the result of whatever odds and ends of paint we could scrounge. Most importantly, though, it was our special place because no sane adult would ever risk getting up into it.

There were real toys, of course. I had a Lionel train set that came out of its box every Christmas, and my friends had Lincoln Logs and an Erector Set. There were toy soldiers made of real lead. You could buy a kite and lots of string for less than a quarter, and someone gave me a tin motorboat with a windup motor. My Uncle Bill made his eldest son and me really neat wooden rifles with moving parts powered by a big rubber band.

The introduction of bicycles into our lives substantially expanded our territory. There were boys' bikes and girls' bikes. The girls' bikes had an open frame to accommodate skirts or dresses. Mine was a bright red American Flyer with lots of chrome. The first shaky ride on "Big Red" is still a vivid memory, as are all the gouges and scars I earned sliding around gravel corners on my butt.

Contemporary bikes do not have fenders, and that trend may have started back in the late 1940s when most of us removed them. The modification came, in part, because badly bashed fenders got caught on big front tires. But we also found the absence of fenders made it easier to fasten little pieces of cardboard to the fork to flap against the spokes making a motorbike-like sound. Mostly, however, it was just a lot of fun riding in the rain with cool water spraying up from both wheels.

Nearly all the roads leaving the village crossed Duck Creek. Several of the bridges were concrete, but many highway and railroad crossings in the county back then were old iron bridges painted silver. There were also a few wooden covered bridges left over from the days of the horse and buggy. The little community of Olive was east of Caldwell along both sides of Route 78. On the east end of that cluster of homes a road crossed Salt Run Creek and headed south to Middleburg. The old silver bridge there was one of our most favorite swimming holes.

On hot humid summer days, a caravan of bikes would head out East Street, race over the bridge at Duck Creek and scoot along the flats to Olive. We would pass the turnoff to cemetery hill and then an old mill on the right. The narrow road turned into a tree-shaded lane separating small white houses on either side. Beyond the homes, around a slight bend, one could see the Middleburg Bridge standing in the summer sun reflecting bright sunlight off its silver beams. Underneath, cool brownish water flowed between large concrete abutments. Abandoned bikes lined the grassy creek banks and kids of all ages splashed about. The more daring ones grabbed their nose and dropped fifteen or twenty feet from girders down into the water.

There was no bathhouse, chlorine, diving board, system filter, chrome ladder or lifeguard. There were water snakes, cows, rocks, snags, horses and probably some fish. I do not recall towels, shoes, or bathing suits. Most of us wore cut-off jeans or shorts. During the daytime, at least, there was no skinny-dipping. But, the dark stream masked whatever the older couples might have done as they huddled with only their heads above water.

By contemporary health standards, the Salt Run swimming hole would be considered a disaster area. The nearest real swimming pool was twenty miles away in Cambridge, and at some point our parents started taking us there. It was certainly more sanitary and safe, but the chlorine was irritating and the rough concrete abused our toes. There was no grass, precious little shade, and we missed having frogs around. The diving board was fun, but not nearly as exciting as jumping off the Salt Run Bridge.

The swimming pool rules specified that one was to take a shower before and after entering the pool and that made absolutely no sense to us. We did not consider ourselves dirty before going swimming and we certainly were not dirty following hours in the water. Besides, like it or not, most of us had a real bath once every week or so.

Often I found myself yearning for the freedom of the old swimming hole where, to my knowledge, no one was ever seriously injured or drowned. But, you would not convince a contemporary County Health Department it was safe.

Growing older, our activities broadened and shifted. The Boy and Girl Scouts offered youth programs and many kids got involved in 4-H, or with the Future Farmers of America. A lot of us were sent off to church camp with mixed results. But probably the most significant change we encountered growing older was the simple realization that boys and girls were indeed different. Consequently, the concept of playmates stepped up a notch. Hanging out at one of several restaurants on the square became popular. Money from mowing lawns, or other small jobs, went for cherry cokes, playing a pinball machine, feeding a brightly lit jukebox, buying comic books or going to Saturday night movies.

Webster defines puberty as, "the stage of physical development when secondary sex characteristics develop and sexual reproduction first becomes possible: in common law, the age of puberty is generally fixed at fourteen for boys and twelve for girls." Pre-puberty, therefore, must be the age when a boy decides being with a girl is nice, but he is not sure why or where it goes from there. So, it was an awkward age. Youth events at the VFW hall featured boys on one side of the dance floor staring at girls on the other, all too shy to get together. I have a hazy recollection of being coerced into taking a ballroom dancing class where boys and girls actually held hands and each other.

Music and dancing became a major part of our high school days. It was the big band era with Glen Miller, Artie Shaw, the Dorsey brothers, Harry James, and a host of other great swing ensembles. It was also a time when the City Services Band of America broadcast Saturday night radio concerts. The high school band introduced many of us to the world of music. And I, like many of my peers, sat down once a week with a lovely lady who patiently tried to teach me how to play the piano with little measurable success.

Growing into early teens, our territories further expanded with access to automobiles. Several buddies had Model T Fords. Most of our parents had automobiles or trucks that could occasionally be borrowed. Gas was cheap and roads narrow, and we began to venture beyond the immediate shelter of our little community. The bridges on old Route 21 were like medieval ramps dropped to cross a protective moat. Over those we went, out into the surrounding world, frequently to the nearest bar in a nearby *wet* township. But, access to store-bought liquor and beer is another story.

Most of the back county roads were unpaved, and negotiating them on a wet day, or in snow, often led to sliding sideways into a roadside ditch. It was not unusual to run out of gas on some country trail. On one such foray, we *midnight requisitioned* what we thought was gasoline from a rusty old tank in the middle of a farmer's barnyard. That ancient Buick nearly got us back to town before the diesel fuel totally gummed up the engine. Fortunately, it was not our family car.

The delightful fantasies and games of childhood faded as we grew and matured. Dating and church activities occupied some; paper routes, part-time jobs, high school sports and the pool hall engaged others. Not surprisingly, most of us grew up to be healthy young adults. A goodly proportion went off to college and into professional careers. Unlike our grandchildren, we did not have Sesame Street, organized soccer, Barbie Dolls, Little League Baseball, G.I. Joe, MP3 players or personal laptops wired to the world. But, we did have imagination and the encouragement to be creative.

Life in the 21st Century would eventually surround us with all the modern marvels we did not experience as children. Yet, I would not for a moment trade the technologies and societal structures of today for the freedom and imagination we all shared growing up in the Noble County hills.

NOBLE HILLS

BOOZE & BUDDIES

For many of us, the right of passage was growing old enough to buy beer, or be with someone who could. Olive Township, and therefore Caldwell, was dry, but it was an easy four-mile drive north to Belle Valley and access to several bars and a state liquor store. Buying beer legally required reaching a minimum age verified by a valid driver's license. But, if you had an older buddy, drinking could, and did, begin at a young age.

Belle Valley was by no means the only source of booze. Lots of little roadhouses did business along back county lanes. Homemade brew was common, so hard cider, apple brandy, wine and pretty good liquor could be had most anytime. Clear, hundred-plus proof whisky was visually unnoticeable in party punch. But, for those who drank the liquid refreshment, its potency was obvious soon after the second glass.

My parents, and many of their friends, drank alcohol. Somewhat regularly my mother, father and I would drive up to Clyde Harris's bar in Belle Valley after the store closed. We would park outside and my father would bring us drinks to have in the car. Mother usually had a beer, I got an old-fashioned green-bottled coke, and my dad drank bourbon and water. Years later, my buddies and I would make the same drive, sans parents.

Many of us also started smoking early in life. Cigarettes were cheap and easy to get. Chewing tobacco was common and, in some forms, enticing to a young lad. So-called "plug" tobacco looked a lot like licorice. A buddy and I tried some once unaware you were *not* supposed to swallow the residue. The results were ugly.

Somehow, we all thought swigging beer and puffing smokes was really macho. And none of us had any sense that either activity could be detrimental to one's health. Drugs might have existed in the area at that time, but I did not see, nor know of anyone, doing anything stronger than alcohol.

Charley was my older buddy. He was a couple of years ahead of me in school and old enough to buy beer and drive his parent's new Studebaker Champion. Those who recall that car know, on a dark night, it was not easy to tell which way it was going because the front and back looked a lot alike.

Two or three of us would join him aimlessly driving about drinking beer. It was a really nifty vehicle and one of the first cars I remember having an in-dash radio. The strains of Johnny Ray singing *The Little White Cloud That Cried* still ramble through my mind. Understandably perhaps, there is no clear memory of really being drunk, but I do recall what it was like to pee on an electrified fence.

Most of us survived that era. Many of my friends went onto college and successful professions. Others stayed in the village and had very productive lives. My love for music, and summers working at the local weekly paper, started me on a long and rewarding media career.

In those young years, it never really occurred to me that our little village had a caring and guiding spirit. There was a New Year's Eve at a bar in Belle Valley when the publisher of our local paper recognized my tipsy condition and volunteered to take me home. Fortunately, although embarrassed, I accepted the offer with his promise not to tell my mom and dad, which of course he did.

Then, early one morning, somewhere along those lonely four miles from Belle Valley back to Caldwell, Charley and the Studebaker went off the road. He died that night, and a lot of us struggled with the incident for many years, deeply saddened by the loss of a great friend.

I have often thought of Charley and what happened to him. Years later I would better understand the nature of fate. Were it not for that publisher, and others over time, it could well have been me along that lonesome stretch of Route 21.

A House on North Street

THE MIGHTY HUNTER

In the 1940s and 1950s, young boys often got a Daisy BB gun at some point in their childhood. Red cardboard tubes of BB pellets were cheap and it was fun to shoot at things. Sometimes rival gangs shot at each other, but that was rare. There was no trash collection so glass bottles and tin containers were plentiful. Both served as targets.

Hunting was a popular local activity and having a BB gun frequently led to a 22-caliber rifle or a small shotgun. My buddies talked of hunting with their fathers or family members. I never quite understood why killing an animal was fun but, having never done so, I could not challenge their statements. In fact, I secretly envied the excitement and camaraderie of it all.

My father did not hunt and did not encourage me to do so Consequently, I progressed from BBs to a single shot Crossman air rifle. It took a lot of hand pumping, but one could get sufficient pressure in the air chamber to drive a lead pellet through a tin can at some distance. The Crossman, therefore, had better range and accuracy than the Daisy.

Perhaps thinking of my buddies tracking wild animals in deep forests, I elected one spring day to go bird hunting down along Duck Creek. The area bird population was significant and included everything from crows to sparrows to red-breasted robins.

Marching confidently down to the end of Main Street, Crossman over one shoulder and pellets in both pockets, I climbed over the fence into Mr. Ball's field and headed for the creek bank. The stream was lined with big old high trees generally full of birds. As if stalking a lion on the Serengeti Plain, I cautiously moved from tree to tree using exaggerated little steps while scanning above for an appropriate target. High in the third tree I saw a big plumpish bird, its dark shape outlined against a lighter green background.

Taking careful aim, I slowly squeezed the trigger. Pffft went the Crossman. Splat went the pellet, and thud went the bird when it plunged to the ground. To my utter amazement, I had hit the damn thing.

With mounting apprehension, I hustled over to my victim only to discover it was not dead. Its little breast pumped up and down, and I could clearly see where the pellet hit its wing. I just felt awful and did not know what to do. Sitting down, I stared at the creature, wondering what in the world had prompted me to shoot it. Then, to better see the poor thing, I lay down on my stomach, placing chin in hands and elbows to the side.

Minutes passed before the bird shook its head, opened one beady eye and peered up at me. It lay there blinking ever so long and then unsteadily got to its feet with a significant wobble. Now, nearly at my eye level, the small creature stood there, looked directly at me and frowned as if to say *why did you do that?* Without thinking, I answered, "Geeze, I didn't mean to," and then quickly glanced around in embarrassment.

Watching the bird soar up into the freedom of a deep blue sky, I swore to never again shoot at a living thing. Many, many years later that oath would come to mind while firing an M-1 Rifle on a Marine Corps target range where I was being trained to shoot people.

NOBLE HILLS

ALL ABOUT SEX

It is hard to believe how naive we all were about sex and sexuality. Had a famous British Prime Minister described the young male sex phenomena at that time, he might have said, "Never have so many focused so much on something they understood so little."

I have no childhood recollection of discussing sex with anyone who actually knew what it was about. The topic was never raised at *our* dinner table or in any public school class I attended. The guys talked a lot about sex and girls, but most of those discussions were pure speculation. Indeed, farm animals had more knowledge and experience than we did.

Frankly, I don't know whether girls thought about guys and sex to the degree, or in the same context, guys thought about girls and sex. I expect mothers talked to daughters on the topic much more than fathers talked to sons, but I also suspect many parents were nearly as inexperienced as their children. Consequently, not a lot of information got passed from adult to child, but a great deal of misinformation was passed from kid to kid.

Associating girls with sex did not just happen on a Monday morning in April. For me, at least, the concept evolved over time. Interestingly, the base of my early thoughts about sex and girls was *numinous* in nature. Webster's New World Dictionary describes numinous as, "having a deeply spiritual or mystical effect," and that was certainly me and most of the guys my age. We would sit around and chatter about how pretty and nice a young lady seemed to be. Secretly, we each had a youthful desire to find out what it meant to be intimate. But, deep down, we had no clue how to get started, or what to do once we got going.

I expect there were some boys who viewed girls as a tool and a means to a selfish end. I do not think that was the case for the male friends I knew well. In our earliest thoughts, we had no clear idea what "the end" was anyway. And by the time we figured that out, we began to understand meaningful sex was far more than a physical thing. But in the early years, we thought, wondered, speculated and, not so patiently, waited for something to happen.

In reality, the era and a highly protective community probably contributed to our sexual immaturity. For instance, as a young boy, I became aware of condoms. I had a general idea what they were for, but I had no idea where they came from. Such things just were not discussed openly. Years later I learned condoms could be purchased in drug stores. But, there was no way I was going to ask any clerk I knew, especially a female, for a package of condoms. It was probably this conundrum that triggered the idea to sell prophylactics in men's rest rooms from dispensing machines. For a mere quarter one could purchase an exotic, erotically colored condom to carry around just in case it was needed. Most of us did so, but in my early years, it never was.

Isolated as we may have been, it was possible to find a sexy clue here and there. One could huddle in a dark corner of the public library and skim through *National Geographic* magazine photos of naked native peoples. Those particular issues always seemed to be more worn than others. Or, one could scrounge through the trash behind the local drug store. Unsold magazines were thrown away minus their covers. If you were lucky, you could find a copy of *Popular Detective*, or something similar, featuring a mature woman with a torn blouse and an exposed bra strap. That image left a lot to one's imagination. But in the late 40s and early 50s Esther Williams in a swimsuit was about as racy as it got!

The source is not clear now, but early on young boys were told it was sinful to "pleasure yourself." The "m" word was not used, and the warning was often ac-companied by an implied consequence. We were told, "If you do that awful thing, you'll go blind." Well, it did not take long for the boys to test the truth of that admonishment, and most of us survived to be reasonably competent visionary fathers who rarely, if ever, discussed sex with our children.

One of the earliest sexual encounters I experienced happened in the old high school building. Grades seven through twelve attended classes there, and the scene between sessions was always chaotic with kids of all ages and sizes madly scrambling up and down stairs and through corridors from one classroom to another. I was in the seventh or eighth grade and following a group of older girls as we climbed steps to the second floor. Suddenly, without looking, one of them reached back, grabbed and fondled me. I was so shocked I failed to identify who it was. I am positive it was a case of mistaken identity, yet for a fourteen-year-old, it was a most exotic experience.

The quest for sexual awareness was a continuing one. Aside from *National Geographic* photographs, there was really no easy way to see what a naked woman looked like, or how girls differed from boys. Buddies who had sisters sort of knew, but their explanations were fuzzy at best. For many of us, the first clue was found in the pool hall. It was located in a damp smelly basement on one side of the square and was a bastion of male chauvinism. In that dim interior, many young village boys first encountered pornography in the form of playing cards or little cartoon booklets. The cards portrayed naked women in various poses and the drawings depicted sexual encounters. *Ah-ha,* we all said to ourselves while closely examining the explicit material, *so that's what it's all about.*

For the temperate village souls, the pool hall was probably considered a den of inequity. Some of its more colorful characters swore, smoked, drank heavily and did not hesitate to pee in the back of the outside stairwell. But this was also a time when school biology books did not contain male-female illustrations, (at least in our village), and sex education was years in the future. So, for many of us, the old pool hall was a place of male bonding and information. In the best of all worlds, one should not learn sex from a cartoon book. But we did. And, along the way, several of us turned into pretty fair pool players, if not expert lovers.

Our quest for female nudity continued in other ways. The high school band frequently traveled to Cleveland to perform at professional football games. On one of my first trips with the band, we stayed in a lovely old downtown hotel. It was not long before the boys discovered a burlesque theater nearby. My buddy and I decided going to a girlie show would be smashing good fun. We slipped out of the hotel unseen by adult chaperons (we thought) and walked to the theater. There, we stood under the marquee's bright lights gawking at posters of nearly nude women before approaching the ticket counter.

Much to our chagrin and disappointment, we were denied admission. It did not occur to us we were much too young. After all, our chins nearly reached the outer edge of the ticket window.

A combination of factors contributed to our placing older girls on a kind of idyllic sexual pedestal. There was a tendency for younger boys to equate a female's physical development with sexual maturity. Now, we know that is a dangerous presumption, but back then we often dreamed of being seduced by a beautiful voluptuous senior girl. Somehow, I suppose, we thought the older woman would know what to do and we would just follow along.

Growing older, we began to understand there were variations on the sexual theme. It was said proper people did not experiment with technique. But, I vividly recall one young lad speculating on an older couple's date. He said, "You know they did it the Chinese way." We would all nod in the affirmative hoping no one ever asked us what that meant, and I never did find out.

The phrase "make out" was commonly used by older boys to describe a dating experience. One would ask, "Did you make out?" The answer was always "Yes." On one such occasion, I got brave enough to ask, "Well what did you do?" His response was "Oh, you know, the usual stuff." And so on. I finally understood no red-blooded American boy was going to admit making out might have only involved holding hands in the front seat of a car.

Over the years, our understanding of sex matured. The early preoccupation with pure physical factors slowly evolved to include a growing awareness of sexuality and social responsibility. The message became quite clear: encounters leading to pregnancy also lead to marriage. So, we were told, you had better be serious about a relationship *before* you go too far along the sexual path.

Mostly, our dreams of seduction never turned into reality. Certainly, some youth became mothers and fathers in high school and some eventually married. Others participated in the joy of sex and went on to different relationships. But for most of us, meaningful sexual encounters did not occur until much later in life. The vast majority of young men I knew talked about sex far more than we ever experienced it.

WHOOPS

Getting to the Noble County Fish & Game Club on Seneca Lake involved taking Ohio Route 78 through Sarahsville to Mt. Ephraim and then to the east end of the man-made lake. On a hot summer day, it seemed to take forever to reach the cool waters for a few hours of swimming.

The NCF&G consisted of an old wooden two-story house perched on a modest bluff above the lake. A smallish barn and several nondescript outbuildings stood nearby, and two huge military-surplus pontoons floated down in the lake. The big rafts were anchored along the bank to serve as a dock for boats and a place for young swimmers to play.

Chasing girls and tossing them into the water was a major pastime. The pontoons were soft, slippery and ringed with heavy ropes. When the girls tired of the silly game, they would withdraw to the bank and watch the boys push each other off the floats.

During one of those pleasant summer afternoons, an event occurred that has remained forever in my memory. It must have been when we were all in high school because the girls were physically well developed.

Typically, we were horsing around having a grand time and picking on an especially pretty young lady who, if not thrilled by it all, put up with our juvenile behavior. Over the side she would go, holding her nose and screaming. Climbing out with the help of many male hands, she would grasp the top of her bathing suit, tug everything up and then prepare for another dunking.

But, one trip up the side of the pontoon did not turn out as expected. Somehow the top of her bathing suit got caught on the rope, and she came up out of the water nearly naked. The suit had been stripped from her chest and almost off her buttocks. Before any of us could react, she stood there bare from the waist up, immediately turned bright red and pulled the suit back where it was supposed to be while we boys looked away in embarrassment.

No one said anything, male or female, but the guys were thinking pretty strongly about what we could not help but see. For most of us, it was our first exposure to near total exposure. I have often wondered if the girl was as upset as she let on, or whether she really understood that, for some of us, it was our first encounter with unadorned female anatomy.

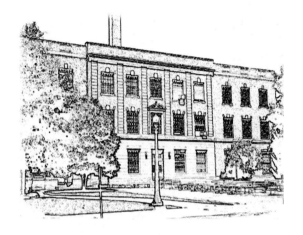

Noble County Courthouse

MARLENE THE MAGNIFICENT

I was in love; absolutely, positively, totally in love. I looked deep into her eyes, and had I known the word *sultry,* I would have thought that. She was so beautiful in a revealing silver-sequined costume, her long dark hair draped casually over bare shoulders. A touch of rouge darkened each cheek nearly to the color of her ruby lips.

"My, ain't she something," my buddy, Tim, said, breaking our trance.

In bold letters, the poster proclaimed the Cole Brothers Circus was coming to town and my new love, Marlene the Magnificent, would perform high on a trapeze. But the advertisement promised much more. There would be daredevil riders, wild animals from the deepest of Africa and, for the very stout of heart, a two-headed calf, a bearded lady, and a giant Tibetan.

Most of us ten-year-olds had never seen a circus because our village was much too small to attract major shows. Yet, there it was, the Cole Brothers Circus was coming to Noble County and right to my hometown.

"We got to go, Tim. We just got to go. How much does it cost?"

"Don't know," Tim answered, scratching an unruly mop of hair. "Maybe your Uncle Jimmy knows."

"Yea . . . he'd know. Let's find him."

Uncle Jimmy was unpacking wallpaper rolls in the back of Hill's Store. Greeting us with a smile, he said, "What's up?"

"The circus is coming and we got to go."

"Yea," he replied. "It was in the paper," his tone suggesting we should not limit our reading to when school was in session.

"What's it cost?"

"Depends."

"Depends on what?" I challenged.

"How you get in."

"Can we sneak in?" Tim asked.

"Likely not," Uncle Jim chuckled, "But there's other ways, and I'd say the matinee for you guys would be fifty cents each."

Our hearts dropped below our bare feet. Fifty cents was a lot of money and we were perpetually broke. "Oh geese," I sighed.

"Or . . ." he drawled, waiting for our attention. "You might work your way in."

"What-cha mean?" Tim asked.

"Well, when I was a kid, I worked to get me a pass."

Tim and I looked at each other; hope springing anew. "How'd we do that?"

"Be first in line when the show comes to town."

Smiling, we knew we could do that and raced off to scout the location, leaving Uncle Jimmy with his wallpaper.

The circus was to be at the high school football field down on West Street. Not knowing when it would arrive, our plan was simple: we would hang around until we saw the first vehicle and be first in line for work. The sun had barely topped the eastern hills when we peddled onto the field, a green grassy pasture with Duck Creek running along one side.

The first sign of the circus was subtle. At mid-morning, a big black Pontiac, burping white smoke, rolled to the field's edge and stopped. The door opened revealing a portly gentleman wearing a gray fedora, black suit, yellow tie and scuffed white shoes. Stepping out, he glanced around, strolled about and then ambled back to the car where he stood patiently puffing on a big fat cigar. Minutes later, the first vehicle of a large caravan rumbled down West Street. The cigar man spoke to each driver as they slowed and then moved by.

Huge noisy trucks and shiny silver travel trailers spread out over the field maneuvering into position with military precision. The travel trailers clustered in one area, trucks with animal cages in another. The last vehicle was a gaudy semi-truck, a garish sign identifying it as "The House of Freaks" featuring the giant Tibetan Monk.

"What's Tibet?" Tim asked, reacting to the sign.

"Don't know. Maybe it's a city . . . or a state somewhere."

"Yep, could be all the way the other side of West Virginia," Tim speculated. "But where'd that cigar guy go?"

We spotted him standing in the middle of organized chaos and watched as he structured his temporary little kingdom. The suit coat was now off revealing bright red suspenders looping down over a significant belly. The stub of his cigar bobbled when he talked and then he noticed Tim and me approach. Without removing the cigar he growled, "Yea?"

Looking up, I stammered, "Ah . . . could me and my buddy . . . err maybe work to . . . ah get in the circus . . .?" The cigar stopped moving, and I thought it was all over, or he was deciding whether we were big enough to help. Finally, he spoke. "You got to see Big Tom." Pointing with the juicy cigar end, he continued, "He's the fellow with the black cap by the generator truck." Looking where he pointed, we saw a huge man talking with other workers. Thanking the cigar man, we headed to the black cap guy.

Big Tom was a giant. Cut-off shirtsleeves exposed immense upper arms, each bicep sporting an elaborate tattoo. Below the black leather cap Tom's face was deeply creased and tanned. His belt had a large metal buckle, and he wore jeans that covered the tops of silver-studded black boots. Sizing us up, he said we could each get a pass if we helped put up the big tent. I beamed at the thought of seeing Marlene, my new love, but neither of us had a clue how much work it would be.

Following Tom's directions, we struggled to help pull great rolls of canvas and big wooden poles off a long flatbed truck. Casually, we peeked at the circus workers. They were middle-aged men who appeared pretty scraggly and constantly smoked cigarettes. Occasionally, they would yell at one of us to do something, or to pay attention to what we were doing. Their language was colorful, even by our standards.

With effort, the big center pole was moved off the truck to a spot marked by Big Tom. Standing there, we wondered what would happen next. Then we saw our first real live elephant. It was immense, even larger than a horse. Of all things, a small girl guided it along with a hooked pole, talking quietly to the animal as it moved.

Big Tom motioned us to get out of the way as he and his workers grabbed guide ropes on either side of the big pole. A hefty hemp line was run from the top end of the mast, through a pulley, to a harness on the animal's back. With little effort the elephant plodded forward, causing the great center pole to slowly rise into the air. When it was vertical, Big Tom whistled and the elephant stopped. Guy ropes were staked in place and the process repeated to hoist up the middle of the tent.

Small posts would support the outer edge of the canvas, and our job was to hook the poles in grommets and hold them in place while guy ropes were secured. An older man, seemingly oblivious to the world, ambled along with an armful of two-foot steel stakes. When Big Tom nodded, the worker kneeled, held a stake out as far as he could reach and looked the other way. Big Tom then tapped the top of the stake with a huge mallet and, with one explosive *ka-bang*, drove the spike two-thirds into the ground. Thinking of John Henry's legend, we worked our way around the big top until all the sides were in place.

Tim and I were dead tired. What little energy I had was sustained by my vision of Marlene. Toward late afternoon, Big Tom gave Tim and me our passes. Just when we were leaving, a lady in a slinky gown arrived to watch the high rigging put in place. Her wet hair wrapped in a big white towel, she walked about pulling on ropes and testing trapeze lines. It occurred to me much later the lady was probably Marlene in civilian clothes.

The next day, we arrived an hour early for the two o-clock matinee sporting our cleanest clothes, Sunday shoes and hair plastered-down with Wild Root Cream Oil.

It was just possible Marlene would fall in love with one of us right that afternoon.

Sawdust and wood chips covered the ground, forming paths to various attractions. Black, electrical cables snaked about providing power to tents and concessions. Hustling to the big top, we proudly displayed our passes and raced inside for the best seats. Before us, three rings divided the center area, one large and two smaller. Slowly the bleachers filled, and a group of clowns bounded through velvet curtains opposite the tent entrance. Their dress alone was enough to generate hysterical, nervous laughter. Next, a troop of brightly costumed people riding one-wheeled bikes, raced into the ring. They chased the clowns out and then, resplendent in high boots, royal blue riding trousers, a bright red coat and a tall black top hat, the Ring Master materialized and began introducing acts.

The afternoon passed quickly. Arabian horses, a small herd of elephants and skilled jugglers sequentially occupied the center ring, followed by a wild animal act. Tigers, leopards and lions worked to the crack of a long whip and the commands of a skinny guy in a safari outfit.

Finally, to the accompaniment of a drum roll, Marlene the Magnificent was introduced. A bright spotlight drove a blazing circle onto the dark velvet curtains at one side of the big tent. We held our breath until Marlene stepped through the drapes, her silver sequined body sparkling in the brilliant light. Long dark hair flowed down her back almost reaching petite slippers that matched her costume.   I blushed when she stared straight at me.

Gracefully she moved to the center ring, shrugged off a ruby red robe, placed one hand through a loop in a dangling rope and majestically floated to the very top of the tent. An attendant began to move the rope in a slow lazy arc, swinging the sequined lady in a great floating circle until she was twirling nearly horizontal.

Once stopped, Marlene climbed to the rigging's highest point and patiently waited for a safety net to be set. Then, she did things on a trapeze I would not have thought possible. We screamed and clapped as each stunt was performed. With a final regal flourish, she literally leaped from her perch into a perfect triple flip dive to land feet first on the net and rebound back high into the air. We all exhaled at one time and roared our praise. Almost casually, she grasped the net's edge and flipped down to a standing ovation.

Marlene the Magnificent bowed to each side of the arena. Smiling, she turned our way and my heart stopped. I knew she was looking directly at me when she blew a kiss and disappeared back through the curtains. Tim went off to talk with a cousin while I just sat there, wondering if I would ever see my love again. I supposed she lived in one of those shiny trailers, but I did not know which one, and I did not have the courage to look. For me, Marlene was really magnificent and she would be my true love forever and ever and ever.

Two days later, the Cole Brothers Circus and Marlene left town, and my heart went with them. I moped about, tried to talk Tim into joining the Foreign Legion and generally sulked. Hoping to get their only son back to reality, my parents urged me to join them for the Sunday movie. In a funky mood, I tagged along. The film was "Lassie Come Home." A young Elizabeth Taylor appeared on screen, and instantly I was in love again; absolutely, positively, totally in love.

Tipton's Hardware Store from the village square.

ONWARD CHRISTIAN SOLDIERS

The beat of the drums is slow and deliberate. Thrrrump, thrrump, thrrump -- tump tump, as we march from the high school down toward the village square on a typically warm Memorial Day. Our West Point style wool band uniforms are already too warm, and the parade is yet to start.

Looking smart, we swing around onto West Street and move to the head of a modest collection of cars and people. Parents work to herd young Scouts and Brownies into marching order. Nearby, very old ladies in pristine white outfits nervously perch on the back of a flatbed truck. Almost everyone has a small American flag. Responding to a sharp whistle, the band pauses to let the VFW Honor Guard move to the front of the line.

Eight men march by in tan uniforms with white scarves and leggings. Black boots and shiny helmets shimmer in the early morning light. All wear white gloves. Six of the men have Springfield rifles. Two others carry flags mounted on dark shiny wooden standards. Gold braid dangles from the chrome tipped poles and mingles with the American and Ohio state flags. One end of each standard is tucked into a white chest-harness designed to support the flag while marching. These WW II veterans are still young and in good shape.

Our State Senator and his family ride in a Chevrolet convertible just behind the band. He is followed by a group of men and women from the local American Legion Post and further back, another truck carries a few WWI veterans. The Noble County Sheriff's big black Ford cruiser brings up the rear. Buildings all around the square are decorated in red, white and blue bunting and high above, fluffy white clouds drift about in a deep blue spring sky.

When all the parade units are in order, Mr. Wood, our director, blows his whistle signaling the drums to resume their slow cadence as we head toward the old Olive Cemetery. Villagers stand quietly along the way watching the parade. Turning east onto Main Street, the band begins playing the classic old hymn, *Onward Christian Soldiers*. It is 1949 and most everyone is focused on those who served their country in two great wars and more.

Noble County had its share of family members in one war or another. Most were male, but a few were women. The names of those from Caldwell were prominently and proudly displayed on a large billboard standing on the square's northwest corner. During World War II, small gold star flags were placed in lighted windows throughout the community. Many of the young men and women who fought in WW II made it back. A few returned as less than whole human beings, and some ended their young lives on a Pacific island or a beach in Normandy. It is in the memory of those brave Americans that we march on this warm May morning.

The journey is a long one. The cemetery is several miles from the square. Somewhere along East Street the smaller children and older adults drop off. The Honor Guard, band and parade vehicles continue down by the Produce Company, across the Duck Creek Bridge on old Route 78 and through the flats up the dusty gravel road to our destination. We march to the tap, tap, tap of drumsticks rapping the rims of pearl snare drums. The cadence is slow, our faces red from the uphill march. A long string of cars and decorated bicycles follow along behind us.

The cemetery sits at the top of a modest wooded hill above the village. In loose geometric patterns, granite and stone grave markers thrust through the rolling grass carpet; fresh cut flowers brighten many plots. Young children race here and there unconcerned about where they step and those buried below. Quickly, the gravestones become a playground for the very young, offering something to climb upon and hide behind.

The band and Honor Guard stop in a small grassy area before a little platform with a portable podium. White dust swirls about from cars and people moving on gravel roads and paths. Here and there, beams of sunlight drive through the overhead cover. Folding wooden chairs, borrowed from many churches, sit warming in the sun or occupied by older people swatting the humid air with colorful paper fans.

Slowly the crowd grows, forms and gains character. To one side, the Daughters of the American Revolution gather; they are mostly old ladies whose bluish white hair nearly matches the colors of the spring flowers they carry. Old men in bits of WW I uniforms gather in another area, trying to stand as tall as possible. A few wear medals and decorations from that bloody conflict. Some of the WW II veterans proudly wear all or part of their uniforms. The Mayor and county politicians are obvious, greeting people and shaking hands.

Boy and Girl Scout troops march into the area. Nearly every child has an official neck scarf. The older ones sport uniform shirts with colorful troop and merit badges. Scattered throughout the crowd, the familiar faces of village merchants and their families are recognizable. My father and mother are present standing with their friends. Many people will go back to church picnics and some will listen to the Indianapolis 500 automobile race on the radio.

The Memorial Day ceremony is simple and traditional. It opens with the Star Spangled Banner. Reverend Brown then delivers a long prayer offering thanks and praise for most everyone. Next, an Eagle Scout leads us in the Pledge of Allegiance, and that is followed by everyone singing God Bless America. The State Senator always delivers the Memorial Day speech. His message is probably different each year, but it sounds the same, and the presentation is dynamic and full of patriotic phrases. We all hear the same words, but how we respond to them, and reflect upon them, is different.

For my generation, WW II was a distant event that happened in strange, foreign places. I recall knowing about the war through Sunday night newsreels at the Roxy or Noble Theaters and being horrified at the devastation of London bombings and frightened for fear it could somehow happen in our small village. As children, those fears were reinforced each time the old fire siren screamed during an air raid drill. The playmates we did not like were always the Nazis or Japs. And, we were much, much too young to understand rationing.

We did not comprehend nor understand the deep sadness of violent death. Only a few of us ever knew of loved ones killed in action. And even then, it all seemed unreal. Clearly, the Hollywood heroes shot on Guadalcanal and during the Battle of the Bulge all came back the next week alive and well to fight once again. It was not surprising we innocently wondered if perhaps this just did not happen with all soldiers. But this day, I know differently.

My parent's visualize another war as they listen to the Senator and think back to the early and mid 40s. They remember the sickening humiliation of Pearl Harbor, the defeats in Africa, and the unspeakable horrors of concentration camps. They recall the deep anxiety of missing and losing a loved one and the tumultuous joy of VE and VJ days. Now, on this lovely spring morning, they are supremely thankful the war is over and the world is at peace. Each parent rests in the expectation their children will never again be called to bear arms, not knowing history would prove otherwise.

On this day in 1949, we all deeply believe our veterans are great patriots. We silently remember those who sacrificed their lives in what we consider to be the ultimate battle for freedom and the right to worship a God of our choice.

The Memorial Day ceremony always closes with a military salute and taps. The Honor Guard smartly brings their rifles in place and, in unison, fires three volleys. The sharp crack of each shot startles most of us and frightens the young children. At the end of the third volley, the rifles snap to Port Arms. As the flag is slowly lowered to half-mast, a trumpeter starts playing taps. Each refrain is echoed by a distant second horn. That hauntingly beautiful

sound drifts over nearby hills and valleys and on into
eternity.

> ". . . Day is done, gone the sun,
> From the hills, from the lake,
> From the skies.
> All is well, safely rest,
> God is nigh.
> Go to sleep, peaceful sleep,
> May the soldier or sailor,
> God keep.
> On the land or the deep,
> Safe in sleep . . ." (1)

(1) The contemporary version of taps was first sounded in
July 1862 for the soldiers of the Third Brigade, First Division, Fifth
Army Corps, Army of the Potomac. There are no official words for the
music, but there are a number of popular verses including the two
presented here. [*Day Is Done] The History of Bugle Calls in The
United States With Particular Attention to Taps:* Master Sergeant Jari
A. Villaneuva]

MR. DAHOOD

The last period of the school day was underway. A.C. and I nonchalantly worked to clean up the residue of shavings, sawdust and scrap leftover from eight hours of "shop." Just as I bent down to better guide the dustpan, A.C. vigorously swung the broom, driving a pile of light dirt into my face. He laughed in response to my reaction. "Hey Al, that ain't funny."

Completing our chores, we hunkered down on a pile of wood to rest. Lawrence Nichols was our Industrial Arts teacher. His domain was a large airy room on the ground floor of Caldwell High School. The area was crammed full of wooden workbenches and big power tools. Walking into the room charged one's senses with the mixed smells of shellac, sawdust and oil. Mr. Nichols' task was to teach a bunch of young boys how to make things mostly out of wood. His real challenge was for all of us to finish the course with as many fingers and arms as we started with.

The workbenches each had a big screw vise to hold wood. Hand tools were stored on the wall, each with its own place and painted silhouette. There were all kinds of clamps, some mounted at the end of long pieces of pipe. My favorite was the old fashioned wood clamp with two jaws and opposing screw handles. Turning the handles in opposite directions theoretically opened or closed the clamp, but no matter what I did I could never get it to work quite right.

A.C. and I were pretty concerned. Word was out that Mr. Nichols was leaving and would be replaced with a new teacher. Sitting there, we contemplated what that might be like.

"You ever hear anyone called Subray Dahood?" A.C. asked.

"Nope."

"What sort of name is that, anyway?"

"Don't know," I replied. "Sounds like some foreign name."

"Well, how come some foreign guy is coming here?"

"Don't know, A.C."

"Why don't you ask your dad?" A.C. suggested.

"Yea. I could do that."

My father was president of the Caldwell Exempted Village School Board. Although I knew what president meant, I never did understand why we were an *exempted village.* Anyway, that evening I did ask him about Mr. Dahood. With a pensive look, he asked why I wanted to know. I explained we all thought the new teacher's name was pretty funny. The village had lots of Smiths, Croys, Tiptons, Hills and Balls, but no Dahood, and all the people I knew had first names like Tom, Jim, Bob and Doug, not Subray. Smiling, my father explained Mr. Dahood was Syrian.

Having no idea where Syria might be, or what someone from there would look like, I appeared skeptical. Frowning, my father continued. "Do you have a problem with Mr. Dahood?" Sensing a mood I didn't wish to challenge, I shook my head "no," and went my way suspecting the hiring of Mr. Nichols' replacement might have been controversial.

Our first encounter with Mr. Dahood was revealing. He had thick black hair, equally dark bushy eyebrows and a heavy-set, short body. His smile was ingratiating and his voice soft. Mostly, he seemed to be a friendly young teacher dedicated to what he did. We quickly learned he was bright, well organized and not inclined to put up with much horsing-around.

But, Mr. Dahood's first major challenge was not in the classroom. The real challenge came from parents and other community adults who perhaps did not easily welcome a stranger and his family into their familiar and secure world. The first several years must have been difficult, but his progress toward acceptance was helped by part of his job. In addition to teaching Industrial Arts, he was an assistant football coach.

In 1952, Tom Saunders, with Mr. Dahood's help, coached the Redskins to the Muskingum Valley League championship. Given the great popularity of high school football in rural America, winning the MVL was a major event. McConnelsville was our hated rival and always the final season game. Caldwell won 27 to 7 and the celebration lasted for months, probably years.

I really got to know Mr. Dahood the summer he hired me to help build bleachers at the high school football field. I frankly do not recall whether the project involved all, or part, of the seating, including a covered bandstand. What I do remember is the beginning of a personal relationnship that flourished for many years and the laughter that came from our mutual experiences.

It was a very uncomfortable summer to work outside. Typically, daily temperatures were in the 80s or 90s with an equal degree of humidity. In the project's early stages, we installed support posts soaked in a black oily substance called creosote. Distilled from wood tar, the substance was commonly used as a wood preservative. It was highly pungent and caustic. In a matter of days, our arms were covered with ugly and sore creosote burns.

All of what we built was put together with big nails. Boards for the risers and benches were cut by hand and nailed into place with heavy framing hammers. When one arm got tired, we would switch to the other one. Although predominantly left handed, I learned to use a hammer with either hand.

I learned other things as well. Mr. Dahood was a great advocate of "measure twice and cut once." He was not an absolute perfectionist, but he was precise. His pride and satisfaction in our hard work slowly seeped into my young consciousness. At the end of each day, we would pause to review what we accomplished and discuss plans for the coming day. Those chats nearly always included a kind remark for something I had done well.

It took us a week or so to get the foundation in place and the seat boards installed. Along the way, I began to understand how working together accomplished far more than one person working alone. I picked up some choice language to go along with hammered fingers and slowly gained the skill to saw straight across a marked line.

The official colors of Caldwell High School were scarlet and gray, so the new bleachers would be painted in those colors. The oil-based paint was thick, came in five-gallon containers and was very tough to stir. We decided to do most of the untreated wood in gray and trim everything in red. The gray base went on easily. We slapped away with big brushes trying to keep the paint off the darker creosote and each other. When that dried, it was time for the trim coat.

The red paint was obviously old. Prying the container lid off, we could see a pool of red gooey stuff with a consistency of nearly hardened cement. Above that was a good bit of pale reddish liquid. Clearly, the goop and the liquid had to be mixed into usable paint. We tried stirring it with a wooden paddle only to discover the ingredients would slurp about but would not integrate. Somehow the mixing had to be faster and more forceful. I'm not sure who first thought of the big old drill press, but that is where we went to solve our problem.

The paint container was placed on the counter next to the drill stand. A couple of clamps helped hold the can in place. The drill head was shifted to the side and over the center of the can. Mr. Dahood found a small steel rod that would fit into the drill press. He bent one end into a shallow "L" to mix the paint and put the other end through a hole in the top of the lid and then into the chuck. The motor was set on low as we stepped back to observe our experiment. It looked like it ought to work.

The mixing rod began to turn as the drill press rumbled up to speed. Mr. Dahood slowly lowered the rod toward the bottom of the can and then kicked the speed up a notch. It was working beautifully. The rod was clearly rotating and we could hear the liquid sloshing inside. Then something happened. The can began to jiggle and the top wobble. Before we could get to it, the lid came off and red paint flew everywhere.

Mr. Dahood slapped the switch and grabbed the can. I just stood in disbelief at the spreading mess. Red paint covered everything. It was in our hair, on my glasses, all over the bench and splattered well up the wall and over the floor. With red streaks down his face, Mr. Dahood looked like a painted Indian. I seriously thought about running away.

With a stern face, Mr. Dahood looked around in disbelief and then he focused on me. I don't know what I looked like, but it must have struck him as funny. Slowly, he smiled and then began to laugh. The first thing we did was get the paint off my glasses. Never once was there a suggestion of error or fault.

It took us the better part of that day to clean up the mess. The red paint never did completely come off of everything. But with turpentine, vigorous sanding and a lot of rubbing, we got most of it off everywhere it splattered. There was enough left to do the red trim the following day and that finished the project.

I took one class from Mr. Dahood, but the time I spent with him that summer was very special. What I gained in that informal classroom went well beyond physical skills. He shared his practical knowledge with me and encouraged me to think analytically. Each construction stage was discussed and planned, and I had a great sense of self-satisfaction when the project was finally completed.

It would take a few years, but the village eventually looked beyond his nationality, his religion and his name to accept him for what he was. Sadly, he died at a relatively young age leaving a wife and young son.

For me, Mr. Dahood was far more than a dedicated teacher. He was an extraordinary, kind human being with a great fondness for life and his family. But to a young lad growing up in rural Ohio, the true merit of the relationship was how it evolved and matured. Starting as a foreigner with a strange name, he became a mentor, a great friend and ultimately, someone I would be privileged to call "Sub."

FLYING TIGERS

Rain poured from dingy skies on a lazy summer morning in 1942 as Cary and I sat in Mrs.Croy's garage. We were surrounded by a mixture of smells from old damp *National Geographic* and *Life* magazines, gasoline and moldy wood. My behind was stuffed into a short stack of discarded tires. My buddy sat backwards on a wobbly wooden kitchen chair that was destined for the dump.

Summer storms were a mixed bag. Sometimes it was fun to dash around in the rain and splash through puddles. Other times, the downpour was depressing and just interfered with normal routine, whatever that might be. Had the thunder and lightening not been banging about, we would have been dunking at our favorite swimming hole. Instead, there we sat, contemplating the world through a curtain of water pouring off the garage roof, spattering over dark cinders and now muddy gravel.

Our intermittent conversation eventually got around to a John Wayne movie we had seen Sunday night. "Flying

Tigers" was probably a low-budget affair, but the aerial dogfights were exciting to us. Cary scratched a mosquito bite, grunted and spoke. "Man, those P-40s was cool!"

Thinking back to the action scenes and Tomahawk fighters, I visualized the planes swooping through the air, all guns blazing. "Yea, they really shot up all them old Japs, didn't they?"

Cary made a swooping gesture with his hand, emulating a fighter going up and over into a dive, and accompanied the movement with a static rat-a-tat-tat sound. "You see those Nips get hit and crash?"

Nodding yes, I pictured John Wayne in an open cockpit, leather helmet strap flying in the wind and then the airplane's painted nose and big white teeth prominently painted on a red background. "And those shark teeth . . ."

"Naaagh," Cary said, glaring at me. "Those ain't shark teeth."

"Well, what are they?"

"Tiger teeth you idiot. They're Flying Tigers."

Not the least bit intimidated, I continued, "Well how do you know they weren't shark teeth or bear teeth, or maybe eagle teeth.

"Eagles don't have teeth."

"Well, whatever they are, they're awesome."

That said, we sat quietly wondering if the rain would be around all afternoon. Cary stood up, shuffled over to the big door and peered out. Speaking more to the alley than me, he said, "We just ought to have us a Flying Tiger."

I struggled up out of the tires and joined him. "What-cha mean?"

"I mean we ought to make us a P-40."

"Oh sure," I answered, holding my hand out to deflect water drops.

"No . . . I mean it. We could make a fuselage with wings and a tail and stuff like that."

Now I was getting excited. "Yea, and we could paint it with camouflage paint and have big teeth on the front. We could even be the Flying Tiger Club."

"No girls."

"What?"

"Don't want no girls in the club."

"Why not?"

"There weren't no girls with John Wayne and the Flying Tigers."

I thought about what he said and it was true. The movie did not show any American women fighting in Burma. So, in our minds, that was reality. "But, we're gonna need some help."

"Yea, could be," he said thinking about what I had said. "But, let's see how we do."

As agreed, we met early the next morning on the lower level of the tree house. Cary had found a drawing of a P-40 Tomahawk and we set about to figure out how to build the plane.

Commonly, the basis for whatever we built was a wooden orange crate. Depending on what you added to it, the light rectangular box could become most anything in our eyes. It seemed like it would be easy to do wings with some boards going back to form a tail. The nose was more of a challenge. I thought we could mange that with cardboard and we could use an old stove bolt to hold a propeller up front. Just as we started to climb down from our perch, the girls arrived.

Mary Ann and Beverly both lived near us down at the end of Main Street. Nearly every day we got together at some point. They were a little younger than Cary and me. The fact that they were girls did not really mean much to us at that age. They were just other kids to be around. They wore dresses more than trousers and had long hair that was sometimes fun to pull.

Cary mumbled under his breath, "Damned girls, always showing up at the wrong time." But, he knew better than to use such language out loud because it would get back to his Grandmother Croy with unpleasant results. The two girls wanted to know what we were doing. Cary explained. "We're going to build us a Flying Tiger."

"What's that?" Mary Ann asked.

Cary frowned at her, displaying his exaggerated dumb question look.

"It's an airplane that John Wayne flies in Burma," I offered.

"You gonna fly it somewhere?"

Cary's expression shifted slowly from disbelief to doubt and back to confidence. "Well sure we're going to fly it."

"Where you going to fly it?" Beverly asked.

Cary looked around, pointed up toward Grandma Croy's yard, and answered, "Up there." We all followed his gaze. "And we're going to have a Flying Tiger Club, but only for boys."

Dropping to the ground, he headed up to the yard with all of us tagging along. Cary stopped on the sidewalk and motioned to an especially tall tree. "Yep, that's where we'll fly it."

I looked at the tree wondering how we would ever get a plane up there and how fast it would come down.

The girls ignored Cary's chauvinistic membership remark, knowing perfectly well, girls or not, they were part of the gang, and Grandma C. had her way of making sure we got along, most of the time. Beverly looked at her cousin. "Well, how you gonna do that?"

Neither of us answered. We didn't have a clue how we would fly the plane, so we just tried to appear confident.

Mary Ann looked up at the tree and then over to another one about thirty yards away. "I saw a movie once where a soldier slid down a long wire and into water. Maybe you could do something like that?"

Cary and I just looked at each other trying not to show surprise. Finally, he replied. "Yea . . . well that's exactly what we had in mind. We'll string a line from this here tree over to that one and fly right along the rope."

We all looked from one tree to the other and back. Beverly then asked, "How you gonna get it up there?"

"There's a big ladder at the store we can use," I volunteered. "And I'll bet-cha we can get some rope from old man Estadt up at the Implement Company."

"Yea." Cary added. "We can't have no knots in it. Has to be all one piece and we'll need a couple of pulleys to make it work."

"What's a pulley?" Beverly asked.

"Well, it's this metal thing with a little wheel that has a grove in it and runs along a rope."

"Oh, we got some of those in the back yard on the clothes line," Beverly replied.

"Can you get em?"

"Sure. Mom doesn't do the laundry till next Friday anyway."

The project got underway the following morning. Mary Ann and I found an empty orange crate at Ball's Market and a big cardboard box at Hill's Store. I had a stash of boards from discarded linoleum crates and a small collection of tools and nails. With her help we piled all of this onto my old red wagon and headed down to Grandma Croy's garage. There we found Beverly and Cary. He had gotten a long length of stout hemp rope from the Implement Company he had promised to take back in one piece. The pulleys were there along with an assortment of paint and mostly hard old brushes. We dumped the stuff from the wagon and headed back to find a ladder.

Over the next several days, our P-40 took shape. The bottom of the crate was reinforced and a low seat added. Several long boards were nailed to the bottom to make the wings. A light frame was built out front and covered with cardboard to form the nose of the aircraft. Using a coping saw (and numerous blades) a propeller was fashioned from a small board and attached to the front so it could spin.

We got really creative with the tail assembly. Cary located some old hinges, and using sash cord we designed a system that would move the rudder from side to side and the elevator up and down. The landing gear came from a baby carriage stored in the back of Mary Ann's parents' garage.

With more cardboard wrapped around the tail, our project actually began to look like an airplane, albeit considerably smaller than a real P-40. The painting part wasn't quite as successful. We could not find dark green, or olive paint and our efforts at mixing did not go well. So, this P-40 ended up a sort of a splotchy pink and mauve. But the nose did feature a red mouth with white teeth. And, like John Wayne's aircraft, our fuselage was decorated with little Nippon flags courtesy of Beverly's little sister's crayons. Round tinker toy hubs nailed to the wing's leading edges served as machine guns, and each wing sported a big white star.

The real challenge turned out to be getting the long rope and P-40 in place. We were smart enough to figure out the rope needed to go from high to low and not just straight across from one tree to the other. Our plan was to launch the aircraft down the rope and into a smooth landing on the lower end. We understood if we were not careful, our plane could glide down the rope and smash into the other tree.

Scrounging in the storage shed of the family store got us several pieces of wire. These were attached to the pulleys and, in turn, to the fuselage. The hemp rope was run through the pulleys and to the base of the two trees. An additional, smaller rope was borrowed from a backyard clothesline and fastened to the tail of the aircraft. Using the ladder, we tied the major support line up into the two trees, the high end about fifteen feet up the trunk. Then, the lower end was tied in place just high enough to let the wheels touch the ground as the plane came down the rope. The clothesline was run through another pulley and fastened to the tree. Pulling that rope backed the P-40 up the main support line into position.

With everything in place, we stood back and admired our handiwork. From other movies, we knew aircraft were first flown by test pilots. Mary Ann brought over her largest doll which, although obviously female, we named Duke. The doll was put in the cockpit and the aircraft pulled up to its takeoff position. Beverly did the count down. When she got to zero, Cary and I released the tail rope, and our Flying Tiger flew down the line and into a smooth three point landing. We all cheered. The doll looked a little shook-up.

I am not sure now how we decided who would make the first human flight. It may have been as simple as Cary being the most appropriately dressed, having found an old wool winter cap that looked a little like a pilot's helmet. Or, it may have been that we drew straws. Anyway, Cary was elected.

We backed the plane up to its takeoff position. With three of us holding the clothesline, Cary gingerly got into the small cockpit. That process was a bit dicey because the plane tended to swing on the pulleys. He settled in place and wiggled the controls. The rudder moved from side to side and the elevator up and down. His goggles were made from two canning jar lids fastened together with rubber bands and string. Pulling the goggles in place, he looked down when we called to him and signaled he was ready to go. With a prearranged, "Tally Ho," the rope was released and off he went.

Our Flying Tiger gained speed as it dropped down the line. The pilot was yelling and we were screaming, but watching the aircraft plunge down the rope, I quickly realized we had made one small miscalculation. Cary was a lot heavier than the doll. Instead of coming to a smooth landing, the aircraft hit the ground with speed and at a considerable angle. It stopped, but Cary did not. Our brave pilot flew out of the cockpit, tumbling head over heels toward the second tree. Just short of its substantial bulk, he landed on his nose and just lay there.

We all ran over very frightened at what had happened. Cary moaned and sat up. Blood ran down his smooched nose and dripped from a scraped and dirty chin. A few tears streaked his cheeks. He just sat there and we stood for a moment. Then Mary Ann reached down to help him up. Grabbing his arm caused Cary to really scream. None of us had ever had a broken arm so we did not know what one would look like or how much it would hurt.

Fortunately, we had grown up knowing when there was a problem there was Grandma Croy. I found her in the kitchen and breathlessly told her what had happened. Following me back into the yard, we approached the crash scene and I am sure she understood what had happened. She also knew how upset we were and that yelling at us would only add to our misery. With practiced care she examined her grandson's arm. "I think it's broken," she said as she stood up. "Let's get him to the doctor."

Off we went up Main Street. Mrs. Croy and Cary were in the lead. Walking briskly, her white apron flapping over a patterned gingham dress and her heavy black shoes clacking on the sidewalk. We followed along to the doctor's office. Some folks were waiting, but the nurse sensed an emergency. Mrs. Croy and Cary were swiftly ushered through a door and back into one of several little cubicles.

It was always fun to visit the doctor's office if you weren't sick or had to have a shot. The smell of alcohol and disinfectant was strong. The big old white scales had weights that moved along a track and a metal rod that came up out of the back to measure how tall you were. Little white porcelain bowls stood here and there stuffed with bandages and cotton swabs, and a tall cabinet with glass doors contained all kinds of colorful little bottles. We absorbed all of this while watching our friend disappear through the door. Our attention then shifted to copies of *Colliers*, *The Saturday Evening Post*, *Life* and a bunch of other magazines we only rarely had a chance to see.

About thirty minutes later, the door opened and Cary came out followed by Mrs. Croy. My buddy looked a little arrogant and walked with a swagger. A white plaster cast encased his lower left arm leaving a dark tanned hand exposed. We all rushed to see the cast as he held it up with obvious pride. Carefully printed along the top were the words "walking wounded." It was a badge of courage he wore for the rest of the summer.

The next day Grandma Croy baked a batch of her famous sugar cookies. With cold cider from the fruit cellar, it was a wonderful late morning treat. We sat around her big front porch as she slowly shifted back and forth in the spring glider. Never raising her voice, she commented about how nice the airplane was but suggested it would be a good idea to retire the Flying Tiger.

So we did. The hemp rope went back to Mr. Estadt in one piece and the pulleys to the clothesline. We put the now badly bent wheels back on the baby carriage and hoped no one would notice and returned the ladder to the store.

The orange crate was stripped of its tail, wings and propeller. There it all sat until the following summer when the crate and wood were reassembled into an Indianapolis race car for coasting down the Olive hill. As it turned out, the design was great, except for the brakes.

RAH – DEE – O

Uncle Burton was one of my favorite uncles partly because he was a true southern gentleman and partly because I rarely got to see him. Every so often, he and my Aunt Margaret Lyons would visit Noble County. They would drive all the way from Georgia to Ohio, usually in a new car. The automobile I most remember was a De Soto with humungous fins.

In his later years, Uncle Burton owned a big, dark green Lincoln Town Car which he often drove wherever he pleased regardless of who, or what, was in his way. By that time, Aunt Margaret was nearly blind and, fortunately, could not see the near misses, but she certainly heard the car horns.

Uncle Burton loved radio. With his deep Georgian accent, he pronounced the word "rah-dee-o." He would explain how the rah-dee-o people up north all talked funny and were hard to understand. One day I asked him how folks in Georgia talked and he answered, with a chuckle, "Just like me – ya'll."

Ohio was not, to my thinking, *up north*, nor did I consider Noble County talk funny. But Uncle Burton was pretty strong in his beliefs and the only person I knew who drank double Manhattans with three cherries and paid to have someone wash his car. So, he was probably right and besides, I too loved rah-dee-o.

Sunday nights at home were special because dinner was better than usual and it was a good radio night. Following ice cream with chocolate sauce and peanuts and cleaning up the dishes, we would gather in a sort of parlor room and cluster around the Zenith to listen to our favorite shows. It was a combination radio and record player encased in a beautiful inlaid wood cabinet with a lighted dial and a grill-covered speaker. Below the radio, the cabinet base housed a modest collection of 78 rpm records including recordings of Guy Lombardo and his Royal Canadians.

My father was our official radio operator. Fine tuning distant stations was part finesse, part art and only possible, he would say, with a certain fix of the tongue. Working each side of the frequency, the sound would go from fuzzy to blaring static and back before he got it just right.

Back then, nearly all programming was network and most shows were introduced by a velvet smooth voiced announcer. Sometimes a program would open with a special sound effect. The squeaking door on *Inner Sanctum* and the evil opening laugh of *The Shadow* invariably prompted me to disappear under my bed.

It seemed one never *just* listened to the radio, and most of us did something else at the same time. My mother knitted, mended or crocheted to keep her hands busy. My dad would settle in his favorite chair, fire up his pipe and browse through *Business Week.* I usually sat on the floor surrounded by whatever toys interested me at the moment. If it was winter, we all edged toward an open gas heater, the only warmth in an otherwise cold apartment.

Because radio was so much a matter of one's imagination, it was a very personal communication experience. For instance, what all tumbled out of Fibber McGee's closet was something we individually imagined. The same personal imagery helped visualize the baseball players in Abbott and Costello's classic "Who's On First," routine.

Perhaps because of its intimate nature, radio signature lines seemed especially meaningful. Lowell Thomas encouraged all of us to join him again by closing with "So long until tomorrow." And, Jimmy Durante's classic line, "Goodnight Mrs. Calabash -- wherever you are," always brought a lump to my throat, although I had no idea who Mrs. Calabash was.

From its inception in the 1920s, radio was commercial, but sponsorship seemed less obnoxious and intrusive in those early days. Most programs had single sponsors like Texaco Star Theater, and many products were associated with jingles or special sounds. There was Brylcream's "A little dab'll do ya," and the "Push –pull, Click – click" of Shick's Eversharp razor which could be had for a buck twenty-five with extra blades.

For a young lad in rural America, radio was a magic pathway to a boundless world. The airways effortlessly took me to an Atlantic City ballroom and the big band sounds of the Dorsey Brothers or to a City Services' Band of America concert. It was fascinating to be alone and realize you were laughing out loud at the antics of Spike Jones or cheering Lou Groza during a Cleveland Browns football game.

Before it gave way to television in the early 1950s, radio started to evolve from a national to a regional and local product. What fun it was to join Ruth Lyons and her crew from WLW in Cincinnati at the Ohio State Fair or to actually hear a Caldwell event mentioned on WILE from Cambridge.

With quickening pace, popular radio shows moved to television. Jack Benny, Amos and Andy, Charley McCarthy, Burns and Allen and many more morphed over to tiny, grainy black and white screens. And, in the process, those wonderful mind images we concocted listening to radio just became old memories.

For whatever reasons, I liked Wildroot Cream Oil Charley and when social circumstances required special grooming, I used the product. But, like the transition of radio to TV, I suspect I imagined my plastered-down hair looking far better than it really did.

THE ROCK ISLAND LINE & MORE

Music was part of our daily life. We listened to it, danced to it, prayed with it and many of us played it. Musical expression, in so many ways, was a fundamental part of rural America. The meaningful presence of music in my childhood started on Saturday nights.

Around the village square, stores were busy, traffic buzzed, couples paraded about, and the high school band played concerts. It was only a short walk from our apartment above Hill's Store to the courthouse esplanade where the band performed. Yet I was always ready to go an hour early, urging my mother to *get a move on*, though not quite in those words.

The glorious spring evenings we spent sitting on splintery, green wooden benches listening to Sousa marches and Strauss waltzes will forever remain in my mind. All around us, most everyone tapped a foot or

nodded to the music's rhythm. Some older ladies, thought
to be prim, revealed their true emotions briskly fanning to
the beat of a tune. And, here and there, old gray haired
men snorted in slumped-over slumber.

On a modest patio before us, the high school band
performed in red trimmed gray trousers, white shirts and
red ties. What they did was absolute magic to me. The
sound of horns, reeds and drums echoed around the little
square, rattling about the stately old trees. One wondered if
the lightening bugs loved the music as much as I did.

Sunday mornings were a different experience.
Sunday School and Bible studies were a tad intimidating to
a young tyke. All mixed together were disciples and stories
and scriptures and Jesus and God and gold stars for good
attendance. And yes, there was music. We little ones sang
Jesus Loves Me, This I know. Then, during our lessons, we
could hear the adults sing hymns to the accompaniment of a
wheezy pipe organ. Later, as young adults, we would sing
from the same hymnals.

Sometime during high school, I was hired to run the
sound system for an evangelistic gathering in the school
gymnasium. Hundreds of folks crowded into that hot stuffy
place to hear God's words from a flamboyant preacher
backed by a piano and small choir. It was my first
exposure to the fervor of hand clapping, feet stomping good
old gospel music. Standing alone in the stage wings, I
watched the Reverend really get it going and subtly signal

the piano player. Her left hand began a base beat for the choir to join and then everything grew to a fever pitch, climaxing with screams of *Praise the Lord* and rousing *Aaaa - mens*.

I had never witnessed anything quite like that evening. The power of the music was narcotic and certainly charismatic. The singing continued as dozens and dozens of folks came forward to commit their lives to the Lord. Wrapped up in the emotion of it all, I was tempted, but much too shy to join them.

At a younger age, I yearned for music of another kind. A unique sound constantly filled my mind in anticipation of an annual event. Then finally, on a muggy August day, we would all climb into the car for a ride to the fairgrounds. Topping a grassy hill to park, one could just hear the calliope-like sound of the merry-go-round, the source of my musical thoughts and my very most favorite ride.

To the beat of a drum and clang of a cymbal, the mechanical notes drifted from the center of the slowly circling wooden horses to embrace and call all of us kids. Then, laughter spilling from smiling faces, we would ride around and around dipping up and down while tightly grasping the brass pole, marveling at the flashing lights and fuzzy world whizzing around us. Other rides were faster, bigger, scarier and more physically challenging, but none had the musical charm of that old carousel.

Over time, more and more music came to our lives through radio or from record players. Certain nights were special because of the WWVA Jamboree out of Wheeling, West Virginia and the Grand Old Opry from Nashville, Tennessee. Occasionally, Jamboree stars would tour and come through Caldwell. Performers like Hawkshaw Hawkins, Stoney and Wilma Lee Cooper and the Clinch Mountain Clan thrilled Noble County audiences at the Roxy and Noble Theaters.

Dressed in sequined western coats, tight pants or flowing skirts, cowboy boots and white Stetsons, the musicians belted out song after blue grass song to the audience's absolute joy. The sound was uniquely Appalachian, and the lyrics the prose of country life. It would be hard to find a more spirited reflection of home-grown America.

Jukeboxes and records brought us the big band sound. The Dorsey brothers, Glen Miller, Arty Shaw, Harry James and, indeed, Guy Lombardo were all popular and part of an unforgettable era in American music. A highlight for me was a trip to Buckeye Lake to hear Billy May live at the resort's big band pavilion.

Looking back, with the benefit of hindsight, it is interesting to recall the music we did hear and think about what we did not hear. I would be well into college before encountering a symphony, opera, bolero, sonata, rock and roll or Mariachi music. And equally interesting, is how some recorded music influenced my life and my understanding of a larger, more complex, society that existed beyond my village.

The first record album I bought as a young boy was a multi-disc set titled *The History of Jazz.* The most intriguing song of many was called "The Rock Island Line," performed by a black singer named Huddie Leadbetter.

> ". . . Cats in the cupboard and she can't find me.
> Oh the Rock Island Line is a mighty fine line.
> Oh the Rock Island Line is the road to ride.
> If you want to ride, you gotta ride it like you're flyin'.
> Get your ticket at the station on the Rock Island Line. . ."

Leadbelly, as he was known, did the song with the driving rhythm of a blues guitar and a voice that captured all the years of tragedy southern blacks experienced over time. The emotional depth of his singing was something one felt and never forgot Experiencing Leadbelly introduced me to the very soul of music and started a life-long love affair with jazz of all kinds.

It was with some musical curiosity that I climbed onto a big bus with my parents in 1943 for a trip to Lakeland, Florida to visit my Uncle Burton, Aunt Margaret and their son, Johnny Bill Lyons. Preparing for the trip, it occurred to me I might run into musicians like Leadbelly, but that was not to be. However, I must have heard Al Dexter's *Pistol Packin' Mama* a hundred times.

The specifics are hazy, but there is a memory of being ordered to take dance lessons at a young age. Our classroom was on the second floor of a building along the south side of Caldwell's square. There were perhaps twenty of us, more or less equally divided by sex. The teacher would start her metronome and count, "one-and two, one-and-two," or "one-two-three, one-two-three," as we attempted to fox trot or waltz.

The girls were graceful and competent, the boys clumsy, bewildered and always embarrassed. If nothing else, most of the guys learned some manners and the rudimentary elements of moving feet with music. Eventually, we did learn to dance and decided it was great fun, but it didn't come easily.

There was the awkward and shy stage when the boys sat on one side of the VFW Hall and ignored the girls sitting on the other side pretending to ignore the boys. In time, that too changed and we grew to enjoy gliding around a dance floor to a Glenn Miller tune holding a pretty girl close enough to smell her hair.

Music took a different focus when some of us became musicians. The Caldwell High School band was regionally famous and its annual Spring Concerts well attended. My playing drums in the marching band led to doing so in dance bands. Performing at the Golden Plaza in Belle Valley with Rollie Hall's band, and later forming my own in college (The Blue Notes) was memorable. But my fondest memories come from playing with a small round and square dance band I joined when I was an eighth or ninth grader.

We played a back-country parish circuit that included the small communities of Fulda, Carlisle and Berne. The Catholic churches all had meeting halls where folks could relax and dance on Saturday nights. These were farming families who worked dawn to dusk growing crops along bottom lands and up rugged hillsides. They worked hard and they played hard. Booze was generally forbidden inside the hall but was plentiful outside.

Our small group performed on a modest platform. The caller had a microphone, but nothing else was amplified. We alternated round and square dance music with occasional polkas and a schottische (a form of dance in two-four time similar to the polka but with a slower tempo). There was a piano player, saxophonist, a fiddler and me on drums, all having a great time.

In these rural hamlets, it seemed music was a tonic for life. Couples swirled about to the words of a caller, clicking heels in unison and forgetting life's daily issues. The very young danced with the very old; boys danced with girls and girls danced with girls and no one thought anything was odd.

It was a time to greet friends, tease a cousin, eat homemade cookies and sip hard cider. It was a time to be thankful for family, life, freedom and God. And somewhere around midnight, it was a time to dance the last dance with a spouse, a friend or a lover, often to the strains of *Goodnight Irene* or *Goodnight Sweetheart*. And, sadly, it was a time long ago we can never truly revisit.

OFF TO JAIL

Miss Newton fussed over us, making sure buttons were properly aligned, hair neatly combed, caps straight and socks up. Satisfied we were as together as we could be, she lined us up, small to tall, and with a nod of her chin marched us single file out of our first grade classroom and off to the Noble County Jail.

Our six-year-old minds were not focused on the gorgeous fall day. Distracted by where we were going, several of us wandered out of line as we exited the elementary building and re-entered the procession out of symmetrical alignment. That caused a small delay while Miss Newton rearranged us back into her sense of proper order. Then, once again, off we started down the school ground steps to North Street.

The sidewalk on the south side of the street was uneven and required some care to negotiate. Large tree roots undermined and pushed up some of the green mossy concrete slabs. Trudging downhill, we approached the McGregor home on the right. Peggy's mother was there to greet us from the front porch. Broom in hand, she swept early fall leaves off the large wooden floor. We were not perceptive enough to understand the smile on her face was from knowing where we were going and what we would encounter.

Our entourage paused at the corner of Lewis and North Streets as Miss Newton assumed the role of traffic cop and carefully checked each direction. Standing defiantly in the middle of the street, she waved us across to the safety of the next sidewalk. Now, we were less than two blocks from the jail, our young minds racing in high emotion. None of us had ever been in a jail and most of us only had a rudimentary sense of why it existed. Universally, though, we understood bad people went to jail and good people did not. While we were all pretty sure we were good people, some of us had this nagging sense of doing something not so good, or not promptly doing something we were asked to do and now wondering what were reasons to be kept in jail.

Soon, Ralston's Drug Store came into view at the corner of West and North Streets. Thoughts of Cokes, sundaes, hamburgers and comic books were pushed aside as we rounded the corner. Heading south at a brisk pace, we soon saw the jail building's red brick facade. Then we were there, stopped on the sidewalk staring up at a sign that read, Sheriff's Office and Jail, Noble County. Being one of the taller first graders, I was near the back of the line and thankful others would enter before me.

An older man in plain clothes walked out onto the porch to greet us. Except for his big gold five-star badge, he did not look like a policeman. We guys were disappointed he did not have silver-handled pistols slung on each hip. But he did look sort of mean, and our confidence was not helped when he loudly proclaimed, "You're all going to jail." And we did just that.

Entering through a screen door, we shuffled into a large reception area where Miss Newton arranged us into three rows ascending short to high from front to back. Numbly, we looked around waiting for the Sheriff to speak. Several things quickly caught our attention. There were telephones, but unlike what we imagined Dick Tracy's office would be, there was no radio. Regularly, a deputy would answer the phone or call someone.

A visual office tour revealed bulletin boards overflowing with "Most Wanted" notices and "Reward" posters, some with FBI across the top. We were too far away to clearly see the photographs, but we all conjured up our own evil images based, in no small part, on Saturday afternoon matinees. Mine sported a black droopy mustache, stringy hair, frightful facial scar, missing front teeth and one ear.

We soon spotted a big gun rack on one wall holding an assortment of shotguns and rifles and boxes of shells. Then we noticed the man at the desk had a pistol belt complete with loops for silver bullets. He wore a sort of uniform; at least his pants and shirt were the same color and he had a badge.

A loud "hurrumph," brought us to attention. The Sheriff told us his name was Jum McKee and, smiling for the first time, he talked about what he did and what the jail was about. Our simplistic understanding boiled down to *catch the bad guys and put em' in jail.* He then told us how we could be good guys and that boiled down to *mind your parents.*

After a few of our questions, the Sheriff asked Miss Newton to form us into small tour groups. The front row marched off with Mr. McKee while we waited. Some minutes later, group one returned and row two moved out. The kids in the first group looked pretty somber, if not on the verge of hysteria. We tall folks just stood there becoming more apprehensive by the second. Then it was our turn.

The Sheriff led us back though large steel doors and along a darkish corridor with detention cells on either side. Big solid bars formed entrances to the cells. We all looked for prisoners but did not see any. The corridor ended at a large metal door with a small sliding steel window near the top. The Sheriff explained this room was special for really,

really bad guys, and wouldn't we like to see what it was like? Most of us thought *no,* but we were afraid to say anything and in we went.

Reluctantly, our small group shuffled through the opening. Before we could turn around, the door slammed behind us with a loud permanent clank followed by the sound of the latch sliding in place. Quickly, all eyes focused on the little square of light coming through the window and then, with a final clunk, it slammed closed. Our dank, dingy and scary little world went totally dark.

Deep down, we all knew this was just a tour, and we would soon be out of the cell. One minute went by, then two and nothing happened. Some of us began to remember things we should have done, but did not. Another minute went by and I was thinking hard about the Sheriff's comment on minding parents and wondering if *not* cleaning one's room could be a punishable crime. Then, with a startling clang-bang, the door opened.

Squinting in the bright light, I could just see Miss Newton's comforting smile and knew all would be okay. We trooped back down the hall and politely, if not enthusiastically, thanked the Sheriff before heading back to school and a lunch of tomato soup with bread and butter sandwiches. About twelve years would pass before I once again met the Noble County Sheriff and entered the jail.

There was no single reason why I got to know Don Conway. He was a feisty half-pint of a man who took guff from no one and was elected Sheriff around 1952 when I was a junior in High School. He married Helen Johnson who, with her mother, lived across Main Street from us above Dack Blake's plumbing shop. Since I knew Helen, it was sort of normal to get to know Don. And by that time I had been working at the paper for several summers and was beginning to get into local news, including what went on at the Sheriff's office.

My hanging around often involved sharing the jail's front porch with Don and Helen on warm summer evenings. We would sit and chatter, sip iced tea and watch the world go buy along West Street, frequently waving at folks going in and out of the Home Restaurant next door. In time, the relationship extended to occasional forays with Don in the department's black Ford cruiser. I do not recall the engine size or how fast it went from zero to sixty, but it did go like hell and riding in it, with the siren wailing and red lights flashing, was a super thrill.

Monitoring traffic and enforcing the speed limit on major Ohio roads was mostly the responsibility of the State Highway Patrol. But, county sheriffs often helped, and it was not uncommon for Don to patrol stretches of old Route 21 in Noble County.

At the time, US Route 21 was the major pathway from northeastern Ohio down south into the hills of West Virginia. The interstate was yet to be built and come Friday night, hundreds of workers from Akron area rubber plants picked up beer and headed home, roaring down the winding two-lane roadway. Typically, by the time some passed through Pleasant City and into Noble County, the back seat was full of empty beer bottles and their speed was well above the posted limit. On this particular evening, we were parked on a little side road near the village of Coal Ridge watching a steady stream of lights flash by.

Prior to speed guns, establishing excessive highway speed was just a matter of tailing someone and monitoring the speedometer. Fast and variously encumbered drivers could be identified by how they negotiated curves. Picking speeders simply involved deciding which vehicle to stop. And once charged, it was most unusual for the judge not to take the word of the arresting officer.

The speeder Sheriff Conway selected was driving a big old Buick with West Virginia plates. It went by in a blur, and with the cruiser's rear tires squealing, we gave chase, lights flashing, siren screaming. The speedometer zoomed past eighty-five before we caught up with the Buick and herded it off to the side of the road.

Don picked up his ticket pad and flashlight, exited the cruiser and motioned for me to stay back near the front of the Ford. Watching him approach the driver I could clearly see two guys in the Buick's front seat and hear what was being said. The Sheriff focused his light on the driver and drawled, "Well now, you boys were movin' along pretty good." Then, motioning to the driver, he continued,

"How about you just get out here with your license where I can see you."

The driver laughed and in a slurred voice said, "Hey, little man, you ain't big enough to make me do that." Then, turning to his companion, he started to speak but paused when he saw his friend's eyes grow large. Turning back toward the Sheriff, the driver looked directly into the business end of a .357 magnum revolver two inches from his nose. At that distance the barrel opening must have looked like a cannon.

Sheriff Conway did not smile when he quietly asked, "This big enough?"

The driver gulped, and with a quiver in his voice, politely answered. "Yes Sir, that's big enough . . . that surely is." Slowly removing his license, he continued to stare at the pistol. The cruiser's revolving red lights cast an eerie glow, causing the .357's barrel to rhythmically flash red.

Given the condition of the driver and his companion, the Sheriff elected to haul them back to Caldwell rather than let them drive anywhere. Handcuffed to each other and the cruiser's back seat, they caused no problem.

Following a quick booking at the jail, the prisoners were escorted through the outer doors into the detention area and down to the corridor's end. The big steel door was opened and then closed behind them. The solid clunk of the steel shutting and the latch sliding in place jogged my memory. My first visit to the Noble County jail came to mind and, as the small window slammed shut, I remembered Sheriff McKee's warning to us first graders, *bad guys do go to jail!*

Noble County Jail Restored as a Historic Site

HIS HONOR

It was a typical Southeastern Ohio fall day with brilliant yellow and gold leaves winking and flashing against a deep blue sky. The air, still warm and moist, stirred occasionally as cars whizzed by me along Route 50 near Coolville, Ohio. I was hitchhiking back to Caldwell from college, hoping to restore some sense of personal identity.

Coming from a small high school in a little village, Ohio University seemed immense to me. As a freshman, I had joined hundreds and hundreds of other kids milling about in a foreign, bewildering and seemingly uncaring, environment. The old adage of "little fish – big pond," was true. I would not have survived that first year without the support of my parents and a gentleman who become a friend of mine and a mentor for many us growing up in Caldwell.

The truck driver dropped me off at the corner of West and Main Streets a little after noon. Thanking him for the ride, I headed for Hill's Store to see my mother and father, and then it was off to find Bud Ralston at the Rexall Drug Store. He was for me a continuing source of encouragement and counsel. I will never know for sure whether he consciously wanted to help people, but that was a continuing byproduct of his personality.

Bud's family moved to Caldwell in 1934, the year I was born. He started working at the drug store while in high school. That was probably when I first knew who he was, but my earliest memories of the Rexall Drug Store do not include Bud. They do include images of chocolate and cherry Cokes, Pearl Ralston (Bud's mother) comic books, *Life* magazine and an occasional hamburger.

I was in grade school in 1943 when Bud enlisted in the Marine Corps, went to boot camp at Parris Island and then headed to the Pacific and Okinawa. He was discharged in 1946 and returned to Noble County along with hundreds of other veterans. That fall he enrolled at Ohio State University and lasted for eight quarters before returning to Caldwell in 1948 to help his mother run the drug store.

At some point in the early 1950s, my motivation to go to Ralston's began to shift. Initially, it was a place to hangout with other kids. We would all cram into a booth, focus on ourselves, blow straw wrappers at each other and ignore the adults.

Perhaps typical of the time, many of us lived our daily lives without really thinking about how a village functioned. We understood there was some sort of governmental infrastructure that kept things in order and working. Somehow the streets were fixed, water came out of faucets, traffic lights functioned and school happened, but *how* was not our concern.

Later, as a budding young journalist, I began to recognize the dynamics of daily life at the drug store and how that related to the overall community. Most everyone of local importance stopped in for coffee or a Coke sometime in the morning. Conversations were informal, often lively and very frequently consequential. In reality, not much happened in Caldwell that was not first discussed over the marble counter at Ralston's.

Bud always seemed to be in the middle of most of what went on. He would stand behind the counter, one foot propped on something out of site, a coffee cup in one hand and a cigarette in the other. Behind him, a plain black telephone rang regularly. His smile was frequent and ingratiating, his outlook positive and his input constructive. Day after day, the business of the community took place along a soda fountain where coffee cups were rarely empty for very long.

It's fair to note that many people contributed to what Caldwell was and would become. The American pioneer spirit was still very much alive in the 1950s. If something needed to be done, folks pitched in to do it. The project might have been a new fire truck, beautification of the village square or helping the high school band get to a Cleveland Browns football game. It seemed Bud was often a catalyst for moving something forward and a willing volunteer to help get it there.

Yet, however busy or involved he was, he never failed to greet me with a smiling "Hi Wes, how the hell are you?" And that is what I looked forward to on that fall day in 1953. Instinctively, he seemed to know when I or my friends were troubled, although at that age our emotions were largely transparent.

On that day, we talked about the loneliness of being away from home, the challenges of new endeavors and our continuing struggle to understand who we were and where we were going.

Bud would cite his own experiences in the Corps and later at Ohio State. He encouraged me, and others, to finish college and not drop out as he did. He helped us realize becoming an adult was as much a matter of assuming responsibility for ourselves as it was just growing older. And he laid the foundation for understanding we each had an obligation to return to the community some of what it gave to us.

My relationship with Bud grew closer when he convinced me to join the 77th Special Infantry Company, Marine Corps Reserve unit in Zanesville. He had a new

Kaiser automobile then that I thought was elegant. Regularly we would drive up through Cumberland and Chandlersville to spend an evening training. Afterwards, we would stop at a Zanesville VFW for a beer and huge bologna sandwiches.

Contact became less regular when I headed off to college and essentially moved from Caldwell. I graduated, got married, finished a graduate degree, went into the Army and on to a professional media career, but from occasional village visits, the local paper and friends, I kept track of Noble County happenings. I knew Bud married Bev Kline in 1954 and that his mother passed away in 1962. I knew he was active in the VFW, Volunteer Fire Department, Chamber of Commerce, Masonic Lodge, Booster's Club and Retail Merchants Association.

Years later, I would look back to those days and my relationship with Bud. Over time, I came to understand all communities across America, large and small, had someone like Bud who quietly and unassumingly helped others. So, it was no surprise to learn he was elected Village Mayor in 1992, a fitting culmination of his many years as a community leader.

On one occasion, I stopped by his City office and noted the sign by his door. It read, "Bud Ralston, Mayor." Remembering the visit later, it occurred to me a more fitting and lasting title would be: *His Honor: Caldwell's Ambassador to the World.*

Caldwell Municipal Building and Mayor's Office

CALLING "CQ"

The cuffs of my jeans were frozen and my feet numb as I tossed copies of the *Zanesville Signal* onto nearly dark front porches down along Cumberland Street. Nearing the end of my newspaper route, I would pass the Nichols' home always wondering why the huge antenna was planted firmly along one side of a small outbuilding. Sometimes I could see Mr. Nichols sitting there doing something but I could not tell what.

Lawrence Nichols was the Caldwell High School Industrial Arts teacher, and most of us boys took his classes. On one school afternoon, my curiosity got the better of me and I asked him what the antenna was for. He told me it was for his "ham" radio rig. A crazy thought of music for pigs flashed in my mind. Seeing the strange look on my face, Mr. Nichols went on to explain two-way amateur radio and invited me to stop by someday after school and so I did.

The inside of the small outbuilding was cozy warm and crammed with interesting stuff. Mr. Nichols called it his "radio shack." Black boxes with dials, knobs, glowing red lights and wires purposefully running about filled much of the space. Along one side, a worktop held a radio transmitter and microphone. Nearly all the wall space was covered with what looked like post cards.

Mr. Nichols motioned for me to sit on an old padded kitchen stool as he dropped into a battered wooden office chair. Little metal casters squeaked when it rolled about. I watched while he turned on, and began to tune, his rig. As the dial moved through bands and frequencies, sound tumbled from the speaker – jumbled voices, static and dots and dashes. Eventually, he found what he wanted and started calling, "CQ, CQ, CQ."

Later I would learn "CQ" was a standard way of calling other ham operators. The term dated back to the days when two-way radio was done with Morse code and letters were transmitted as a series of dots and dashes. Some say, CQ was a way of saying "seek you."

I became fascinated with ham radio and would sit for hours as Mr. Nichols chatted with other operators hundreds or thousands of miles away. They would exchange pleasantries back and fourth, always concluding with phrases like "over," or "back to you." Frequently, conversations dealt with signal strength, reception and the local weather.

It was customary for each contact to be validated through the exchange of post cards bearing the operator's call letters and documentation of date and time. Some cards were plain with stamped information, but others were elaborate and colorful. Those on the walls of the shack ranged from shiny new to old and faded.

Sometimes Mr. Nichols would let me make a call. Not having a license, it may have been improper for me to be on the air, but no one challenged us. Eventually, I asked Mr. Nichols what one had to do to become a licensed operator. He explained the Federal Communications Commission requirement included being able to receive and send messages in Morse code. I tried, but never progressed much beyond SOS, (. . . - - . . .) the international distress signal.

Becoming more familiar with the transmission process, I realized ham radio signals skipped or bounced off the hemisphere and often traveled great distances. It was not unusual to contact someone on the East Coast, in Canada or even Europe. Where the contact was made soon became a kind of game for the two of us. Mr. Nichols would ask, "Do you know where London is?" If I did, and could properly identify the location, he would place a small gold star on a little framed world map he had made for us. If I did not know the location, it was my assignment to look it up and report back.

Somewhere I acquired a small dented metal globe that colorfully portrayed world geography. Unfortunately, it was not large enough to identify many major cities by name and I would turn to the school encyclopedia for information. Finding a city often led to reading its history and dreaming about being there. Forays from Caldwell were few and usually not far, so places like London, Lima and Paris seemed light years away and forever beyond my reach.

Slowly, my interest and knowledge of the world grew with each ham radio contact. We would sit there mentally soaring over invisible airwaves to distant, and for me, exotic places, never in my wildest imagination expecting I would visit them.

But over time I did, and upon arriving at those far-flung and still exotic destinations, I often found myself thinking about Mr. Nichols and his amateur radio. For it was that mystical little black box with its big antenna that first transported a young Noble County lad to Canada, South America, France and beyond.

PRINTER'S DEVIL

My professional media career began the day Clarence (Bober) Estadt, the publisher, and John Wheeler, the editor, offered me a summer job at *The Journal and Noble County Leader*. The opportunity to earn money and work for a newspaper while in high school was so compelling, I agreed before knowing what a printer's devil did or would be paid. Turns out it was a nifty title for a back shop "gofer;" the pay would be five dollars and fifty cents a *week*, and it would be years before I really had anything to do with reporting or writing..

The tasks I enthusiastically, if not skillfully, tackled focused on the mechanics of printing and distributing two papers a week (*Journal* and *Leader*), helping on small commercial printing jobs, cleaning black ink off of everything including myself, and making what seemed like a hundred thousand little white scratch pads.

Early on, one understood a goodly amount of printing and publishing in the 1950s was done by hand.

Small presses were used for job printing, and getting blank paper onto the printing surface and printed material back off required skill, rhythm and deft handwork. A much larger flatbed press was used to print the newspapers. It was a noisy mechanical marvel that transformed huge rolls of newsprint into individual newspapers. The entire building vibrated when the big press ran, making normal conversation impossible. When, for whatever reason, the wide sheet of unwinding newsprint broke, all hell let loose and I would learn a few new swear words.

Printing, of course, involved letters, words, sentences and paragraphs. Individual letters were gathered from type cases to form headlines or advertisements and sometimes text. Type for newsprint came from weird looking, clattering machines called Linotypes. A melting lead ingot was fed into one end of the device and column-width lines of words came out the other. Pictures and illustrations for stories and advertising came from engravings and cast lead plates. All of these elements were combined and locked into page-sized steel frames for use on the big press.

Before moving the pages, everyone helped space and tighten the forms and carefully lift one end of each frame off the composition table to check its integrity. The first one I lifted fell apart, dumping all the classified ads on me and the floor.

When not involved with publishing and mailing the papers, my work turned to job printing tasks. We did everything from business envelopes to county fair premium books to raffle tickets. At that time, items like tickets had to be hand-fed into a printing press, hand-numbered, hand-perforated and hand-stitched into books. I got involved after the printing and was assigned to hand-number the tickets with a little stamping device. I was doing just fine until someone noted the number on the tickets did not match the number on the stubs. Fortunately the error was caught before the tickets were delivered.

To my great good fortune, a wonderful gentleman named Leonard Long took me under his wing. Although Bober and John *thought* they ran the back shop, Leonard really did. He was quiet, very skilled, mostly patient, highly professional and extremely dedicated. Under his tutelage, I learned a great deal about printing, journalistic composition and interpersonal relationships in a workplace.

In his unassuming way he introduced me to the concept of front office and back shop worlds. He never really characterized the differences as "we-they," but in response to my questions, his answer would be, "That's the way *they* want it," or "That's the way *I* want it." Leonard would not suggest a front office edict was necessarily wrong, but he would offer what he considered a better way to do something. Or, he would quietly suggest a particular story was lean on fact and hard on editorial opinion.

For many years, Mr. Long was the sports reporter for the paper. Caldwell was then a member of the old Muskingum Valley League that included such schools as McConnelsville, Philo, New Concord and Crooksville. Leonard would travel with the team over narrow, crooked back roads, often in terrible weather and never, ever complain. On occasion, I would help him record basketball game statistics, and that experience introduced me to the importance of keeping accurate reporting records.

That first summer flew by rapidly. Learning was sometimes painful and embarrassing. In spite of Mr.Long's guidance, I once got the stitching machine so entangled in wire it had to be disassembled. The big paper cutter blade was continuously nicked because I would forget to move a metal ruler out of the way. And the Post Office frequently returned papers whose mailing address had been mangled by my inept use of a truly diabolic labeling machine. But I must have done more right than wrong because both back shop and front office folks encouraged me to continue. And after several summers as a printer's devil, I was promoted to the front office and yet another adventure.

The first day of my new assignment as a news-person, I crossed Main Street, walked into the paper's main entrance and stopped. Normally, I would have paused long enough to greet everyone before heading back into the shop. Now, for the first time, I looked about the work area with some curiosity and a lot of confidence. After all, I had completed my second year toward an Ohio University journalism degree and knew absolutely everything there was to know about writing and editing. Or so I thought.

Knotty pine paneling gave the room a warm feel, enclosing an area that included a glass counter by the front door and a bunch of office desks. Each workspace had a Royal or Remington manual typewriter and stacks of paper piled around, under or on black telephones. Most of the desktops had overflowing ashtrays contributing to a perpetual haze of blue cigarette smoke drifting under an acoustical tile ceiling. Large windows on the north side looked out onto Main Street.

My journalistic activities actually began when I was still in the back shop. The Caldwell High School Band was extremely popular at that time, with a regional reputation. John Wheeler knew this and encouraged me to write a weekly column about band activities. I believe it was a *Columbus Dispatch* reporter who first tagged the band as "Marvin's Musical Marchateers," after its innovative director, Marvin Wood. In a variation of that theme, my column title became "Musings of a Musical Marchateer."

A review of those early columns suggests whatever readership they might have generated came totally from interest in the band and not from my personal writing skills. But the assignment got me started and introduced me to newspaper deadline requirements. It also introduced me to a fundamental journalistic concept not clearly emphasized over four years of a college degree program. Under John Wheeler's guidance, I began to understand the importance and value of local news.

Those early reporting assignments consisted of re-working promotional releases from agencies like the Farm Bureau and County Extension Office. Then, I was assigned to edit correspondent stories from outlying communities like Coal Ridge, Crooked Tree, and Derwent. Most of the correspondent letters were hand written and difficult to read. They would report something like, "Mr. and Mrs. Joe Jones and family recently visited with Mr. and Mrs. Yardley Gamberolkoskie last Sunday afternoon." I had no clue whether the information or spelling was right or wrong. Eventually, John Wheeler graciously suggested I might become a fair writer, but he advised me never to seek an editing job.

Over time I progressed to covering local events and writing original stories and, eventually, a weekly features column. I especially remember covering and writing about the Firemen's' Festivals, spring floods, fatal auto accidents on Route 21, strip mining, village council meetings, county fairs and local elections. Along the way, I learned the paper's community affairs involvement often went beyond conventional reporting. Bober Estadt was very active in a range of village activities and particularly supportive of economic growth and quality of life issues.

Bober's articles occasionally assumed an advocacy viewpoint, something my journalism professors considered unacceptable on a newspaper's front page unless labeled "opinion." That bothered me some until I figured out that, in the context of supporting positive change, such writing was perfectly acceptable wherever it was placed. And, as publisher and co-owner, he could do whatever he wanted to do, but it was mostly okay because readers understood why he did it.

My introduction to photo journalism happened when a picture had to be taken and both Bober and John were busy doing something else. Bober handed me the big Speed Graphic, mumbled something about "f-stops" and sent me on my way, neglecting to tell me the cover sheets from the 4 x 5 film plates had to be removed *before* taking pictures. Whatever that event, it did not end up as a photo in the paper.

Photo journalism was mostly fun and sometimes exciting. I recall wading through floodwaters with the Graphic held high above my head, suspecting the camera was considerably more valuable than I was. On another assignment, I found myself perched precariously at the very tip of a huge earth-stripping machine because I thought it would be cool to shoot down the boom to the bucket. The picture was interesting, but it had not occurred to me the wheels and cables at the tip would be liberally coated with grease. Getting back down without slipping off or losing the camera was just dumb luck.

Close to the end of my tenure with the paper, I badgered the bosses into buying a new Ford car to use for deliveries and reporting. The sedan was light gray, very plain and a standard shift. It was a great ego trip for me to roar up to some news event, "Press" card prominently displayed on the windshield and Speed Graphic firmly in hand. I suspect a few state troopers and local politicians chuckled at my Clark Kent enthusiasm for journalism.

The front office stint lasted several summers and was a marvelous learning experience. We all did a little bit of everything, and I had my turn at advertising design and sales. My artistic abilities were mixed. I had a good sense of composition and balance but only marginal execution skills. The logo for Wehr's Clothing that I designed was different, but amateurish in form. Graciously, Dick Wehr used it anyway.

When I left Noble County to pursue a full time media career, *The Journal* followed along. Like thousands of other former residents, the paper was my weekly link back to Noble County. It rarely carried a story of earth shaking consequence, but as its motto proclaimed, it covered Noble County "like the sunshine." The featured stories would be about a basketball game in Batesville, a school board meeting in Caldwell or a soil conservation tour near Summerfield. Wedding anniversaries, birthdays, family reunions and college graduates all got mentioned.

Compared with the large metropolitan papers I would read as I moved around the country, *The Journal* often seemed outclassed. After all, the big dailies did not carry death notices or classified ads on the front page. Nothing in the local paper was in color then, and *The Journal's* stories did not always follow proper journalistic form.

Over time, I began to understand a fascinating phenomenon in print journalism. Many of the major American dailies merged with each other, existed for awhile and then folded. But every week twenty or so pages of tightly wrapped newsprint would regularly arrive in my mailbox from Noble County. In spite of its small size, something kept *The Journal* going.

It was, and still is, a task to remove the wrapping without demolishing the newspaper and then get it flat enough to read, but we all eagerly did so without thinking much about why *The Journal* was so anticipated. Then one day, reading something in the front section, I remembered a comment John Wheeler made to me years before. It was a simple, but profound statement that defined the continuing success of weekly papers throughout America. "You know, Wes," he said, "local people are mostly interested in local people."

Permian Oil and Gas (left) and The Journal Buildings

WINTER WONDERLAND

One eye slowly opened, then the other. It was totally dark beneath the covers and freezing cold above them on this late fall morning. Unfortunately, knowing what time it was required peeking out of my bedroom window from under layers of warm blankets. Facing east, the window provided a view of the store's tin warehouse roof, homes down at the end of Main Street and a low ridge line beyond Duck Creek. If the sun was just peeking over the hill, it was time to get up.

Frost on the inside of the window distorted my view, especially without glasses. Squinting, I could tell it was still mostly dark, yet the color was not quite right. Wiggling out from under the covers, I reluctantly put on my glasses and started rubbing the frost. Slowly, the view cleared and I gasped because everything I could see was buried under several feet of snow. *Boy oh boy*, I thought, *this is a biggie.*

My mother and father were dressed and eating breakfast when I bounded into the dining room, grinning from ear to ear and not recognizing their somber expressions. For me snow was fun, but for them it was hard work and a pain in the neck. Their day would include shoveling snow, spreading ashes on the sidewalk and sweeping mush off the store's wooden floor. I, on the other hand, could not wait to find my sled and hit the hills.

Insisting I eat a hearty bowl of oats, my mother began her, "I don't want you to catch a cold," lecture. That meant putting itchy wool long johns on under regular pants, layering flannel shirts and sweaters beneath a heavy coat, wearing the cap with the tie-down ear muffs and pulling on big four-buckle galoshes. Heaven help me if I ever fell over, or had to go to the bathroom.

Smothered in clothing topped off with a wool scarf and mittens, I flung open the front door, waddled out onto our upstairs porch and paused in disbelief. Everywhere I looked the scene was absolutely white. I had never seen so much snow nor experienced such an absence of sound. Cautiously peering over the porch railing, I could see empty streets and sidewalks below. Up at the corner by Gillespie's Drugs, a red and green blur flashed through the falling snow as the traffic light did its thing. Very carefully I trudged down the porch stairs to Main Street, my trusty Western Flyer sled thumping along behind and my thoughts focused on the many sledding spots around the village.

Our favorite hill was north of Frazier Street near where Route 285 ran up the valley toward Sarahsville. It was a pretty good slope with a few bumps and no trees until you got down to the bottom and over toward Duck Creek, which was frozen solid this time of the year. Although nothing was ever prearranged, we all would migrate to the same hill at about the same time pulling various sized wooden sleds with steel runners.

Sledding style was mixed. Some would sit, guide the sled with their feet, and bash down the hill with one or two on board. Some would "belly flop," steering with their hands, using feet to brake or slow down, and occasionally we would explore other options. One could use a tin garbage can lid to slide down the hill if you smashed or broke off the handle and did not mind twirling about or riding backwards. Cardboard would also work until it became too soggy and disintegrated. Several of us even tried skiing with barrel stays using tomato stakes for poles, but the results were marginal, moderately dangerous and frequently humorous.

A muffled yell from across Main Street interrupted my thoughts. Old buddy, J.R., dressed just like me, waddled out the front door of the Permian Oil and Gas Company and waved. It was hard work pushing through the snow to the middle of the street, but we met there knowing cars would not be along until a snowplow blasted through, spreading cinders and salt. At least for awhile we would be free to wander about. Nodding in recognition, we turned and headed up Main Street to the village square, frosty breaths leading the way.

The farther we went, the slower we moved. Our progress was measured by the deep drifts and what we experienced around us. Falling snow created a mystical landscape where trees became harsh shadows; lights a mere twinkle, and sound strangely muffled. Pausing at the corner of Main and East streets, we could barely see sparse traffic creeping cautiously along old Route 21 a block away. And down to our right, near James and Quick's men's store, the screech of a snow shovel scraping over concrete rankled tranquility.

Thoughts of sledding on the hill by Route 285 dimmed with the realization it would take us a long time to get there and then disappeared temporarily when accurately thrown snowballs pelted us from across the way. Yelling in youthful delight, J.R. and I charged across the street in search of our attackers. The subsequent battle ebbed and flowed around the Court House grounds for much of the morning with each side reinforced by passing adults momentarily slipping back into childhood.

Sopping wet, noses red, mittens stiff, most of us kids headed home for lunch with the promise of reassembling behind the Main Street Methodist Church to go sledding. The snow continued to fall as we impatiently stuffed down whatever food our mothers provided, all anxious to return to the winter wonderland.

By two o'clock, a dozen or so of us were running or rolling down the hill by the church packing down snow for the sleds. Soon, more tracks were open as the numbers grew. By late afternoon, lots of folks were gliding down the slope, including a smattering of adults, grandparents and toddlers. Fires started to burn here and there as dusk settled and hot chocolate became available. Quickly, it seemed, much of the village population had gathered near the church, either sledding or watching an impromptu celebration that could well have been the subject of a Norman Rockwell painting.

The revelry continued well into the evening. Eventually, youthful energy gave out, the old and very young got cold and people slowly drifted back to their warm homes. My parents, like others, had arrived after work with warm food for me and my buddies. Caked with snow, clothes and pull rope mostly frozen, my Western Flyer gliding behind me, I trudged along in my parents' footsteps thinking about what a wonderful day it had been.

Two mornings later, I lay in bed, covers over my head and nose running profusely. The pungent smell of Vicks Vapor Rub was overwhelming. My pajamas were literally plastered to my chest with the sticky salve-like substance considered by all mothers to be the universal cure for a winter cold. And, to top it off, my misery had just been upped by a significant dose of Castor Oil accompanied by a motherly expression which clearly said, *I told you so.* But, exchanging loving smiles, we both understood: sledding the big one was great fun and the Vicks jar would undoubtedly be opened many more times before winter passed.

COUNTY FAIRS & KEWPIE DOLLS

It is hard to imagine any event in rural America more universally popular than a County Fair. Its blend of activities offers a diversion for many, rewards for some, and when I was growing up, nearly uncontained excitement for us kids. Ferris wheels and merry-go-rounds were no match for roller coasters, but if you threw in cotton candy, hot dogs, soda pop, peanuts and horse racing, it beat most summer afternoons in Noble County.

The old floral hall was an early focus for me because Hill's Store always had a booth and I was recruited to help set it up. The building was structured like a cross with four wings thrusting out roughly along the major points of a compass. Inside, thumbtack-peppered dividers separated various sized areas used for merchandise display, FFA, Grange and 4H projects and an eclectic collection of civic booths. Above an uneven brick floor, naked light bulbs dangled from exposed wooden beams, each dusted with eons of spider webs and bird droppings.

Many Caldwell and area merchants rented space in the hall. Our spot was on the north side of the east wing. My father, uncles and I would go out to the fairground days before the official opening, and while the adults checked the booth, I would scout the rides and concessions. It never occurred to me the location of things would really not change from year to year.

The Ferris wheel was always just across and down a bit from the Floral Hall's west wing and near a smallish white building that housed a food stand. Between that facility and the Floral Hall, a narrow gravel road wandered north for several hundred yards to the animal barns and south down over a hill to one of the gates. The road was flanked by dozens of gaming tents, trailer mounted food stands and commercial displays.

The Hill's Store booth had different products each year. I have forgotten all of the displays except the one year we featured Lowe Brothers' Paint. Gallons and gallons of the stuff were loaded into the store's old blue Chevy Suburban before chugging up Main Street and out Fairground Road to the Floral Hall. I was appointed chief carrier while my dad, Uncle Bill and Uncle Jimmy arranged the cans. Struggling from truck to booth, I could manage two gallons a trip praying fiercely at each step that next year's display would be cotton quilt batting or something equally light.

Although setting up the booth was hard work, it was fun. We would exchange pleasantries with the Murphys as they moved furniture into their area. The appliance store folks carefully wheeled new shiny white refrigerators and stoves into the building while, outside. a caravan of bright green and yellow John Deer tractors lumbered up the hill from the Implement Company.

Before the fair got underway, prize winning vegetables, pies, cakes, bedspreads and wood shop projects appeared on tables running down the center of each of the hall's major aisles. Someone had the enviable job of tasting all the sweets to select the best for an award. Outside, one would find farm machinery, the latest new automobiles and assorted rides scattered over the grounds.

The days immediately before the fair officially opened were frantic ones, and it always seemed to me nothing would be ready. Vehicles of all sizes and types rattled about delivering animals of all sizes and types shepherded by kids of all sizes and types. Somehow, the livestock ended up in barns, stalls or cages while groups of carnival workers magically transformed colorful parts into functional rides. Concession stand tents went up and hundreds of prizes got unpacked and put on display, including red, white and blue kewpie dolls liberally adorned with silver or gold glitter.

As young children, we were free to roam the grounds with little or no supervision, but my mother used her sternest voice to warn my friends and me about the *carnies* It was never clear exactly who that was, why we should not go near any of them, nor what might happen if we did. Consequently, we looked everywhere trying not to stare but doing so anyway. The non-locals we did see appeared a little grungy, but otherwise displayed no obvious reason why they would be a threat to anyone.

The true challenge of the fair was deciding how to spend the few dollars I had managed to cajole or save over months of taking out trash and mowing lawns. One had to prioritize between rides, candy apples, hot dogs, colored ice, or trying to win a prize. Throwing baseballs at little milk bottles, tossing hoops or flinging darts at balloons could result in winning a huge stuffed animal or a glittery doll. But for most of us, riding the rides was the first priority.

Early on, I was permitted to do the merry-go-round by myself, but one of my parents always accompanied me on the Ferris wheel. The excitement started while standing in line watching the seats drop down as the big wheel rotated. Slowly, we would shuffle forward until it was our turn. Using a long lever, the attendant would stop the wheel and step down on something that caused the seat to tilt and shift forward. Then, just as we sat down, the safety bar would drop with a loud clang, the seat would move free, rocking gently as we dropped backwards to the roar of a muffled engine.

Certainly, part of the ride's thrill was the wheel's circular movement and the anticipation of stopping at the very top before dropping down for another cycle. But part of the thrill was just being high in the air, something a kid could not easily do in our village. Maybe the top floor of the Court House was as high as a Ferris wheel, but looking out a stationary window was not nearly as exciting as rocking at the very top of the wheel high above twinkling lights and milling crowd. I often wondered whether Ferris wheels ever got stuck and how one would get down, but I never faced that dilemma.

Well before any of us really understood betting on horses, sulky racing was a fascinating activity. The track, grandstand and barns were over the hill on the east side of the fairground. In between rides and hot dogs, we would run down the grassy hillside past a little white ticket booth to watch a couple of races in the grandstand, if we could sneak in. For many of us, the fascination with horse racing was a combination of factors that included colorful racing outfits, a motorized starting gate, cute carts and the precision of the trotters and pacers.

Horse racing was not the only grandstand event. There were many special attractions, but my very favorite was Joey Chitwood and his daredevil drivers. Blasting about in brightly painted new automobiles, Joey and his folks would launch off ramps, slide about in curtains of dust and race down the track tilted up on only two wheels.

Sometime later in life I considered trying the two-wheel stunt with my father's Buick, but common sense and fear of repercussion prevailed.

The Caldwell High School band frequently played at the fair. We would gather at the north gate, march up the hill to the rhythm of drum sticks rattling against rims and then launch into a lively march as we crested the ridge and headed south toward the Floral Hall. Often, the band would perform a concert and sometimes we would do a precision marching show on the race track, trying not to step in liberal piles of horse manure.

Growing older, priorities shifted from rides and cotton candy to girls and prizes. The better (or luckier) guys won furry stuffed animals or glittering kewpie dolls for their female companions. I, on the other hand, threw baseball after baseball, hitting nothing but the back of the tent. Every so often, one or two milk bottles would topple from turbulent air, but never all three.

Over the years, and a small fortune in quarters, I never did manage to win anything. My frustration grew each August until I finally resolved the problem by buying a kewpie doll. I don't recall the cost, but it was probably appreciably less than what I spent trying to win one. It sat on my dresser for many years resplendent in red, white and blue paint with silver glitter, a continuing reminder of youthful frustrations. Some years later the kewpie doll disappeared, replaced by a fraternity mug and then a tennis tournament award, and then . . .

THE BAND

Just before sixth grade chorus, Mr. Wood, our band director, asked me to stay after class. I worried through the entire hour. What had I done? What had I not done? What was I supposed to do, but had not? The chat was brief, mostly one-sided. Mr. Wood asked me if I would like to be in the band. He thought I would make a terrific tuba player.

A few days before my encounter with Mr. Wood, our football coach, Homer Pyle, invited me to try out for the team speculating that I would make a great tight end. Both options interested me, but the choice was really predetermined. Given my poor eyesight, it seemed unlikely I would ever see a football on a pass route before it hit me. So off to the band I went.

In its case, the tuba was nearly as big as I was. It got from school to home and back on a little red wagon. Although capable of a few umm-paw-paws, I mostly just carried the blasted thing in endless parades. To this day I know there are telephone poles in southern Ohio towns with dents about seven feet up where I ran into them with the horn's bell, smashing my lips with each collision.

Fortunately, my tuba tenure did not last long and I switched to the snare drum, a much smaller instrument. Under the tutelage of Bill Semon and Neil Smith, I learned to be a reasonably competent drummer, and that became my instrument nearly all the time I was in the Caldwell High School band and beyond.

By the time I joined the band, it was already regionally known for its musicianship, precision marching and unique dance routines. The perfection came, in part, from a summer band camp focused on developing and perfecting new formations. The annual two week event was also a time for beginners like me (nicknamed *Rinky-Tinks*) to work into an organization that was beginning to be the pride of Caldwell.

My father and I worked for days preparing for my first band camp outing at the Noble County fairground. The girls stayed in the Floral Hall with Mr. Wood's wife, Francis, and the boys slept in an old livestock barn with no doors, open windows and a dirt floor. It was tradition to create a home away from home. My dresser, orange crate side table, cot and old fashioned steamer trunk were painted the school's colors, scarlet and gray.

The camp spanned two weeks in the middle of Southern Ohio's humid summer. Reveille was at 7:30

A.M. and lights out about 11:00 P.M., although few were asleep at that hour. The per-student fee was under ten dollars, and the entire affair was made possible by a wonderful Band Mothers Club, dedicated parents and contributions from local merchants.

By the end of camp, we were in fine shape for fall football game performances and a slew of regional appearances. Many high school bands in the late 1940s and early 1950s played well, but few could match the marching style and precision of Marvin Wood's thirty-six musicians. I am not positive, but I believe a *Columbus Dispatch* reporter, Bob Wheaton, originated the title, "Marvin's Musical Marchateers." But mostly, we just called it "the band."

The group traditionally performed in a diamond formation. All music was memorized and played without an on-field director. One of the band's more famous routines involved a formation which exploded over the entire football field. Midway through the exercise, no one member was within ten yards of another and then everyone marched back to form the basic diamond. This routine was sometimes done in the dark with small red and blue penlights attached to the band member's shoes.

The band uniforms were a West Point style design. The unit's snappy image was enhanced by white shoes and a tradition that had girls pin their hair under our tall hats. At the time, white shoes were not common and many of us painted brown or black oxfords white. To help assure neckties were tight and neat, Mr. Wood conducted Windsor knot tying classes. Nothing was ever worn over the uniforms except a transparent plastic rain jacket. But, whatever one could stuff underneath was okay for cold outings.

Memories of those band years are full of warm fuzzy feelings, long bus trips, exciting new places, good friends and unforgettable experiences. At the Detroit Police Field Day we dressed in a tent and had to evacuate when it caught on fire from errant fireworks. Our Greyhound bus broke down on a trip to a Cleveland Browns professional football game. Arriving late, we performed after the game, and most of the crowd remained for the show. Planted in the middle of the stadium looking up at nearly a hundred thousand people on their feet in a standing ovation was an experience none of us will ever forget.

Other memories are equally strong: summer concerts on the Court House esplanade, the slow cadence of a Memorial Day march to the old Olive Cemetery, dropping a drumstick on a freezing cold January day in Cleveland, forgetting the words to *McNamara's Band* during a spring concert and the ever pungent smell of itchy wool uniforms on a muggy August day.

As vivid as some memories remain, it is remarkable what one does not recall. In all of my association with

Marvin Wood, I do not remember ever being screamed at, humiliated or openly criticized. I'm sure he must have yelled at us, but it was never personal or vindictive. And perhaps even more remarkable is the realization none of us ever thought the work and time commitment was too harsh or unfair.

Sadly, traditions and institutions come and go. Marvin Wood died from a cerebral hemorrhage in 1960. His dream of taking a small rural high school band to regional prominence was largely fulfilled. In so doing, he instilled a sense of lasting pride in each of us and the understanding that self discipline, dedication and mutual respect are the basic ingredients of success, indeed of life.

In the late 1980s, my wife and I visited friends in Athens, Ohio and dined with them at the Ohio University Inn. Our conversation ranged over many topics, eventually drifting to my high school years and being a member of the band in the early 1950s.

My lively account of band experiences was interrupted by a voice from a nearby table. "Excuse me," a pleasant-sounding female said, "Are you talking about *the* Caldwell High School band?"

Surprised, we all turned to see an older lady looking somewhat embarrassed by her intrusion. "Oh my . . .," she stammered, "I'm really sorry for butting in."

"That's okay," I answered, and then curious, I added, "How do you know abut the band?"

"Well," she said, "We saw you perform in Lancaster years ago and you were just marvelous." Brushing aside graying hair, she went on. "We used to live in McConnelsville and we'd see you during football games when we played the Redskins. I guess we've always been a little jealous of your band. It must have made Caldwell proud to be represented by such a fine group of young kids."

I thanked her for her compliment realizing she could never know how poignant her comment had been. Pride, it seems, is an emotion one never loses.

SHENANIGANS

Except for a few utility lights, the Noble County fairground was nearly black on a muggy August evening. It was Saturday night in the middle of the two-week high school band camp and we guys were fulfilling a long-standing tradition. Our task was to guard all the stuff our fellow band members left at camp over the weekend break. The girls' gear was in the Floral Hall where they slept, and our bedding and clothing was in an old, open, livestock barn.

Our interpretation of the tradition included liberal amounts of alcohol. The preference for drink varied from guy to guy. Several elected beer, some drank Four Roses and Coke and one chap had a thing for Southern Comfort. How and where the booze was acquired is best left unsaid. Being isolated and without wheels, we were only a threat to ourselves.

The early evening chatter focused on whether to invade the Floral Hall for whatever goodies we might find, but the idea faded as the night progressed. Some of us knew it would be an invasion of privacy, of sorts, and some of us also knew anything amiss would point to our presence. Anyway, the hall was locked, and we knew breaking in was illegal, even for a cause we thought acceptable.

Predictably, our conversation turned to girls. Silly thoughts became sillier, jokes dumber and our mood lighter directly proportionate to the declining booze levels. Approaching midnight, our world was fuzzy, our equilibrium shaky and our eyes heavy. Had it been New Years, we would have missed the entire celebration, dead to the world wherever we dropped.

Waking Sunday morning was a disaster. Serious hangovers were not part of our normal experience and we had neglected to plan for anything that might calm unsettled stomachs and pounding heads. Knowing it was the Sabbath did little to clean up our language as we struggled to keep eyes open, legs steady and supper down.

Ever so painfully, visual and auditory capacities returned along with a foggy sense of awareness. Several of us did a head count and came up short. Someone was missing and that was cause for alarm. By ones and twos we fanned out looking everywhere for our lost buddy. Searching other barns and miscellaneous buildings revealed nothing. Then as panic neared, we heard strange sounds coming from a nearby restroom.

Facilities, as they were sometimes called then, came in different sizes. Many village folks had small outhouses with one hole. Public restrooms were much larger, featuring more holes and rudimentary plumbing for the men. Lime was used to help offset the odor.

Approaching the small building, the sound became more distinct. One could hear the trickle of moving water, then a substantial thud followed by a hysterical giggle and then silence before the cycle started again.

Inside, we found our buddy propped in the corner of a tin lined trough extending down the side of the room, a foot or so off the floor. Several feet above his head a wooden box, balanced on a trundle, slowly filled with water dripping from an overhead pipe. When the water level reached a certain point, it tipped the box thoroughly dousing our friend and cascading down the trough to the roar of his laughter. In between each dump, our pal took a long pull from his Southern Comfort bottle, not realizing its content was now only water.

The longer we watched the funnier, and more compelling, the scene became. Soon, we pulled our buddy out of the corner and began taking turns under the dump, giggling in anticipation of the cold shower, and roaring when it came. Maybe it was the ice cold water, or maybe it was the humor, but we all began to feel better.

Daily life in those days was full of remedies for everything from lumbago to hives. Our remedy for a big time hangover worked well, but never made it to the next decade to my knowledge. Fortunately, that facility and its plumbing didn't make it either.

GRANDMA CROY

If you asked me what Grandma Croy looked like, I would answer matronly. If you asked me to be more specific, I could not. Although I received zillions of hugs from her over the years, the image of her face remains an indistinct memory. Yet, for all of us growing up in the 1940s on Caldwell's east side, she was our grandmother by acclamation if not by relationship.

Some of my friends had living grandparents, I did not. My father's father died before I was born, and I have only a vague recollection of his mother in her Brooklyn brownstone, and no recall of my mother's parents. So, as far as I was concerned, Mrs. Croy was my grandmother.

She lived nearly at the east end of Main Street in a large, rambling two-story white house with a porch along two sides. A garage sat on the west side of a tree-covered lot and next to it, a small storage building. The structures and lush grass were play areas for us.

To this day I can recall the rich sweetness of her homemade cookies and the chilling cold of fresh milk from her ice box. She would treat us to glasses of sweetened Cool-Aid on warm summer days and hot cider on cold winter afternoons. Sometimes, there would be a slice of apple or cherry pie for an afternoon snack.

When she existed in my life, I had no understanding of her quiet wisdom, subtle guidance or daily influence on our young lives. She was simply there, sometimes a nurse, sometimes a judge, often a comfort and always a grandmother. Her shaded and cool porch, with its cushioned gliders and metal rocking chairs, beckoned and sheltered us on rainy days and summer nights.

Under Grandma Croy's guidance, our little gang became the champion firefly catchers of all time. She would provide each of us with a small Mason jar, inspect each cap to assure there were sufficient air holes and then send us out into her spacious yard. Squealing and laughing, we would race about in the growing darkness filling glass containers with lightning bugs, pausing now and then to marvel at their flickering light.

Then, at the end of the evening, we would gather around Grandma Croy for a modest ritual. She insisted every lightning bug be released and each jar returned clean and empty, reminding us all living creatures must be free and respected.

Joining her in a little prayer we would be thankful for the good of the day and the love of our parents. And ever so gently, she would remind us the softly twinkling fireflies, now freely flying about, were signs of God's presence in our world.

In a very real way, Grandma Croy and others like her were rural America's guiding matrons. Always caring and lovingly supportive, they gently helped generation after generation grow through childhood to puberty and beyond.

Through all the years Mrs. Croy was a part of my life, I never knew her first name. Over fifty years later a friend would tell me it was Eva, and I am thankful to know that. But, in my memories, she will always be just *Grandma* Croy.

Part II: Going Back

GETTING THERE

I returned to Noble County over the first Labor Day weekend of the new millennium and again in 2003. The trips were made to chat with friends, re-visit old haunts, attend my 50th high school class reunion and explore what had, or had not, changed over fifty years.

Flying to Ohio offers a startling geographic transition from Arizona's parched desert and rugged mountains to the lush rolling hills of the Midwest. Approaching Columbus, it is almost unsettling to see so much green grass and foliage after forty years in the Southwest. There have been, of course, other trips across America, but the pervasiveness and richness of the color continues to be startling.

Through the open window of a rental car heading east on I-70, (forever Route 40 in my mind), comes the smell of fresh cut grass and newly plowed fields. The humidity is high, the traffic heavy and my emotions soaring. Swinging south onto I-77 at Cambridge, I elect to get off the freeway at Belle Valle and take old Route 21 into Caldwell. The chills really begin crossing the Duck Creek Bridge near the water works. Then, cresting the subtle rise that becomes Mill Street and turning south onto Miller, I hear a mystical voice from somewhere deep in my soul saying, *Welcome home Skibo, welcome home.*

IMPRESSIONS

The visits were fascinating, often emotional, and sometimes amusing. Wandering about the village and the county, my thoughts constantly shifted from present to past and back again. For instance, my childhood memory of Hill's Store is of a large impressive structure vibrant with people and commerce. Our upstairs apartment, though far from modern, was spacious and a comfortable home for over twenty years.

On Labor Day 2000, I looked at a shabby old abandoned building rotting under years of accumulated pigeon droppings. And then, three years later, there is no building at all, only a parking lot with a few dusty cars and a couple of pigeons searching for someplace to roost.

Superficially, the village seems much as it was when I lived there as a child and teenager, yet it has changed. R C. Moore's lumber company building along Fairgrounds Road still stands, but the sand pile we so adored is gone, along with the roar of powerful milling saws. The Noble County Jail has become a historic site and the structure looks great, but there are no sheriff's deputies or prisoners there now.

Mrs. Croy's lovely old white house sits quietly down near the end of Main Street and across from where the Quicks and Richcreeks lived, and a new house stands where Mrs. Croy's yard used to be. The pasture we called Ball's field continues to separate the village from Duck Creek, but our tree house is long gone, as is the tree.

Merchants and banks remain on the square, but what they offer differs from when I lived there. Today, only one grocery store remains and shopping for major items, it seems, has mostly moved north to Cambridge or south to Marietta. A hardware store still exists at Main and Cumberland Streets, but the old tin nail bins are not there.

A new village economy clusters around the Interstate 77 exit. Fast food restaurants and large service stations dominate what used to be a quiet little intersection near the Noble County Fairgrounds. The tranquility of that corner has been replaced by the throaty rumble of large semi-trailer trucks rushing off, and back on, the interstate.

Out east, above the Olive Cemetery, modern homes climb up a hillside and perch along a ridge that was just woods and fields when I was a child roaming the area. Nestled in a pretty valley below the ridge, the small community of Olive now offers many new businesses and a lot more stop signs.

Driving through Belle Valley, I note the Golden Plaza and Oasis bars continue to serve thirsty folks. However, the State liquor store has moved somewhere else. But, the greatest change is aesthetic. The huge pillars of an interstate bridge, nearly in the middle of town, seem grotesquely out-of-place against a tree-shaded lane lined with quaint old homes.

There was time to meet and look up many friends. We chattered about years gone by, laughing, and sometimes crying, over faded memories not yet dimmed by failing bodies and aging minds. We spoke of the good times and ignored the bad as thoughts and emotions inexorably shifted back through time.

Walking by the corner of Main and Young streets, I thought of my father and his friends playing tennis on an old clay court where a house now stands. Continuing east down Main Street, I remembered sledding behind the Methodist Church and attending Sunday evening movies at the Roxy Theatre.

Remarkably, the original high school building still stands, although it is only marginally functional, and surrounded by new facilities sporting touches of scarlet and gray. The football field has moved to the Fairgrounds, replaced by a school bus maintenance and parking area.

Casually motoring south along old US Route 21 through Elba, Lower Salem and Whipple generates memories of trips to Marietta and the Ohio River fifty years earlier. And there is a warm fuzzy comfort in realizing all those small communities still exist.

The area continues to be charmingly beautiful with thick forest covering many of the rolling hills. Little white churches still dot rural crossroads and faded old barns still promote Mail Pouch chewing tobacco, although one I saw featured a sparkling new McDonald's sign.

All the people I meet are as friendly and caring as ever and rich in culture, if not comfortably prosperous. Although only a few people call me "Skibo," I find myself on an emotional high from the familiarity of it all and the realization the basis of my fondest memories remains intact

Yet, there is a haunting feeling one can never truly go home after years of being away. I find little things surprising, and sometimes, unsettling. Driving around the square, I realize there are now traffic lights on only two corners and not four, as there once were. The absence of familiar landmarks is sad. Ball's (corner) Market and the Noble Theater are gone. There used to be three or four gas stations in town; now only one remains.

But times change, and unlike some small villages across America, progress has been kind to Caldwell. Flowers are everywhere, streets are clean, trees are trimmed and lawns mowed. The homes I pass are neat and well maintained, and the old brick streets continue to cause tires to chatter.

One evening, lying in bed, I think about all of what I have seen and experienced over two visits. The thoughts are pleasant, warming and remarkably reassuring. Inwardly I smile, remembering the *welcome home* voice I first sensed driving into the village days before. Then I drift into sleep and dream of sailing little ships on little ponds back in '43.

South side of Main St .on the Village square.

SHERIFF SMITH

Landon Smith has been Sheriff of Noble County for years and years. His oldest brother, Neil, and I played drums in the Caldwell High School band together. I believe Neil was perhaps fifteen years older than his youngest brother. To my recollection, I had never met Landon.

Strolling around the village square early one morning, I watched a Sheriff's Department vehicle pull up in front of the old Noble County jail and park just south of a corner restaurant. The car was big and black with a prominent gold star on each front door and a humongous radio antenna off the rear bumper. Old images of the big Ford cruiser Sheriff Don Conway drove in the 1950s briefly came to mind as I watched a door open.

The driver got out and ambled into what used to be Ralston's Rexall Drug store, now the Corner Confectionery. I followed along hoping it would be Sheriff Smith and that I might chat with him about his brother, Neil.

The restaurant's interior is different now, but the black and white marble soda fountain counter is still there. Perched on a chrome pedestal stool was a man in jeans, western boots and a gray shirt drinking coffee and puffing a cigar.

Dark hair streaked with some gray topped a weathered brown face with clear piercing eyes. There was no sign of a badge or a weapon as he chatted with Judy Brown, the restaurant's owner. I sat next to the man, ordered a cup of coffee and asked, "Would you be Sheriff Smith?"

Slowly, he turned toward me and, with a twinkle in his eye, answered. "Yes, and you would be Wesley Baehill Marshall."

His answer so dumbfounded me I forgot to ask him how he knew who I was or, of all things, how he uncovered my middle name. We had a great chat and I commented that it must be election time in Noble County because there were signs all over urging folks to vote for Sheriff Smith. He grinned around the cigar and answered, "That's a pretty astute observation for an old newspaper reporter."

So, not only did he know my name, he knew I had worked for the local paper years ago. He let that thought dangle and then said, "Actually, I just get the signs out every once in awhile to remind folks I'm Sheriff."

I ran into Landon two more times on that trip. At the Noble County Fair he was scooting around on a little black electric golf cart with large gold stars on each side. The second encounter was at a Labor Day picnic. Both events provided the opportunity for him to politic a bit. It all must have been successful because he was re-elected in November, 2000 by a wide margin and started his 29th year in office. He says he's never had a day off and I believe him.

St. Mary's Catholic Church in Fulda

RAILROAD TRACKS

When I lived in Caldwell, the Pennsylvania Railroad went through the village and under the North Street viaduct. The tracks are now gone. There is a modest dip in the street where the viaduct used to be, but no bridge.

Thinking back, it startled me to realize I never exactly knew where the tracks came from, or where they went. Presumably, the trains ran along a line between Cambridge to the north and Marietta to the south, carrying all sorts of freight and, one supposes, passengers in the early days. But that time has gone and the traffic has moved from the railroad's parallel steel ribbons to the interstate's twin concrete lanes.

If you were in Caldwell for the first time driving where the viaduct used to be and looking north, you would see a fairly deep grassy depression bordered by modest tree-lined streets and quaint homes. If you had lived in Caldwell and followed the same route with a nostalgic mind, you would imagine the old steam engine puffing along, black smoke billowing back over a string of cars and a red caboose. And, if your memory was truly sharp, you would recall being there as a young child, feeling the old viaduct shake to the rattle of steel wheels on steel rails, and wistfully wondering how far the tracks went, where they ended and whether you would ever in the world go there?

A LABOR DAY PICNIC

Noble County is rich in traditions. One takes place on the first weekend of September at St. Mary's Catholic Church in Fulda. I was invited to join Pat and Malcolm Parks and her sister, Betty, for the Labor Day picnic.

Rain smeared the Buick's windshield as we headed east on Route 78 and turned onto the Middleburg road. Several miles south, we branched off onto a Township lane heading up into the hills above the middle fork of Duck Creek. Heavy foliage framed each side of the road and nearly arched over us as Malcolm carefully drove along the wet pavement.

Pat and Malcolm have lived in Caldwell for many years. He was a member of the Volunteer Fire Department and is now with the Coast Guard Auxiliary. Pat is with the Historical Society and writes articles for the local paper. Their houseboat is docked along the Ohio River a bit south of Marietta. They are both retired and share a delightful view of life clearly influenced by a marvelous sense of humor.

Driving along, they talked of the farm they had owned in the area and about the cows that constantly got loose and lost in the rugged terrain. And, they softly spoke of the dreams they had of building a home somewhere on that land.

Going back to Fulda was a special treat for me because fifty years earlier I was a member of a little dance band that played in the church's white meeting hall. St. Mary's was one of several Catholic parishes on a circuit we did on Saturday nights. And then I remembered other connections to the community.

When I was a young child, my parents arranged for a Fulda girl to live with us while she attended the last year or two of high school in Caldwell. It was a common arrangement in town because the Fulda school stopped short of the twelfth grade. She helped with household chores and babysat me in exchange for room and board. Then, on weekends, she would return home.

My memory does not include her name or what she looked like. But, I vividly recall the brown sugar pies she made and the occasional visits we had to her home. It was always a joy to be offered thick fresh pork side sandwiches on homemade bread with sweet apple cider from a hillside fruit cellar

Pat's voice snapped me back to the present. She told me the Labor Day picnic commonly drew between fifteen and seventeen hundred people. I wondered how the rainy day would affect attendance and where in the world that many folks could park. As we came up onto, and drove along, a lovely tree lined ridge my questions were answered. In the near distance, the red brick Catholic Church came into view, literally surrounded by shiny, wet vehicles parked everywhere except on top of each other. Malcolm dropped us off and headed out to find a parking place. I wondered if he ever would.

My guests speculated the attendance was probably down some, but it didn't seem that way to me. A substantial line moved slowly along toward the ticket table. Brightly colored umbrellas stood out against a dark sky and a canopy of moist green tree branches. Absolutely no one seemed perplexed or upset with the rain. Indeed, the mood was jovial and friendly. Pat and Malcolm's son and his wife joined us as we shuffled toward a plastic canopy sheltering the ticket folks. Approaching the table, we passed a gray-haired lady selling raffle tickets for a stunning handmade quilt. And that reminded me of Hill's Store and the days when quilts were proudly displayed, hanging from the old tin ceiling.

Moving up a short flight of steps, we entered the Parish Hall. Over my protests, the Parks insisted on paying for all of us. So, I don't know what the meal cost. Inside, one could feel the warmth of the large crowd and smell the aroma of home cooked food. Table after table after table of people filled the room. Our line ambled along one side toward a serving area. Sheriff Landon Smith ate in clear view of all who entered and greeted most by their first name. He smiled at me and I waved.

Nearing the food counter, I stared in disbelief at what all was being piled on plates. There was roast beef, chicken, mashed potatoes, gravy, stuffing and green beans with ham. At the end of that line was another large table overflowing with pies, cakes, custard, rolls, cookies, bread and other wonderful looking stuff I couldn't identify. Supporting my plate with both hands while trying to balance a glass of iced tea, I followed Pat out the back door and under a series of large tents.

We found Malcolm at a picnic table with room for all of us. In the center of the table were large dishes of homemade coleslaw and plates of plump red sliced tomatoes. Eating all of this, I thought, would surely fulfill my dietary needs for months.

A light, misty rain tapped the canvas above us as we chatted and ate. Malcolm pointed out local dignitaries helping to clear tables. I thought about the tremendous effort required to stage an event like this and the volunteer hours required to prepare everything.

Up the soft grassy hill toward the church, a bingo tent was crammed with people. A male voice called out the numbers: B-5, G-3 and so on, until someone happily shouted "Bingo." Down the hill behind us, folks wandered through the old St. Mary's cemetery peering carefully at gravestone legends. The air about us was damp and chilly, tinted with the aroma of fresh cut grass and farm cattle.

For a moment, the conversation paused as our minds seemed to drift away to other times and places. My thoughts refocused fifty years in the past at a Saturday night dance where the people surrounding me looked not much different from those at the picnic.

There in my vision were the folks who managed a living on land difficult to farm. There were the women who bore and raised children in the tradition of their ancestors. These were the ruddy-faced kids who roamed the creek banks, climbed the apple trees and sledded down white winter hillsides.

The Saturday night social was a time to relax, dance and enjoy life. Outside the hall the men, and some of the ladies, sipped hard cider or homemade brew. Inside, grandparents talked and watched their grandchildren bounce about to the lively beat of a country schottische. Young lovers shared moments of intimacy, moving gracefully to the three-quarter rhythm of the *Tennessee Waltz.*

Reality returned with the nearby scream of another "Bingo," but my thoughts continued. Elsewhere in the world, life moved to the demands of a society driven by new technologies and E-commerce. But here in this place, at this moment, life is quieter and more gentle, somehow uncomplicated by world issues. Most of the people around me have spent their lives in the valleys and hills of this county. Many will die and be buried here, but I sense their spiritual compassion and love for life will exist forever.

SUNDAY MORNING SERVICE

The First Presbyterian Church sits at the corner of North and Lewis Streets. Broad front steps climb up to a south-facing double door. The building's red brick frames stained glass windows and supports a modest bell tower. Out front, a glass-enclosed sign in the midst of a colorful flower plot displays coming events, a sermon topic and the pastor's name.

I arrived a few minutes early for service, slightly nervous. It had been over fifty years since I last walked into the building. The sanctuary was exactly as I remembered. Rows of dark wooden pews flowed down a gently sloped floor to a pulpit and a choir area backed by symmetrical brass organ pipes. All about, the light blue interior walls stand in sharp contrast to dark wood trim.

Pastor Susan Highland greeted me, and we chatted about my early days with the church and my writing. Around us a mix of old and young people milled about, settling into their customary seats. Dr. Highland acknowledged my presence at the opening of the service and described the purpose of my visit. Her sermon was lively and motivational, but a collage of old memories clouded my concentration: Sunday School classes, Christmas plays, dress-up Easters, roller skating in the church basement and reluctantly dropping my precious pennies into a wicker collection basket.

Standing for the closing hymn, I looked over the congregation and the beautifully sunlit room seeking what had changed over years. The only difference I could see was the addition of an audio sound system and a few ceiling fans. Otherwise, the bulletin I held in my hand could just as well have read, September 3, 1941.

SWEET TREATS

Growing up, many of us spent small fortunes on hamburgers, soft drinks, and sweets of one sort or the other. My favorites were cherry, vanilla or chocolate Cokes, phosphates and marshmallow milkshakes. Young high school girls working behind the black and white marble fountain at the rear of Ralston's Drug store concocted most of the treats.

After leaving Caldwell, I searched far and wide for marshmallow milkshakes made with real marshmallow and real ice cream. It is easy to find chocolate, strawberry and vanilla milkshakes, but not marshmallow. Part of the problem, I suspect, has to do with contemporary packaging and products. Today, some marshmallow comes from a jar that, when extracted, looks like mashed potatoes moving swiftly toward total rigidity. It is also easy to find milkshakes made from a soft dairy freeze product which has the consistency of two-day old mushy snow.

On the Friday before Labor Day, 2000, I stopped by the Corner Confectionery one morning thinking of a cup of coffee and pie ala mode. Casually scanning the menu to see what the day offered, I was astounded to see marshmallow milkshakes on the beverage list. So much for coffee and pie! I could not resist ordering a shake, wondering if it would taste the same as it did years ago.

From my booth I could see the counter person assemble my treat. Several big scoops of vanilla ice cream plopped into a dented, stainless steel mixing container. That was followed by generous glops of marshmallow smoothly flowing from the fountain dispenser. Then she added a long glug of milk and put everything on a green electric mixer. The final product arrived at my table complete with glass, straw, bright red cherry and long-handled spoon.

Milkshake connoisseurs know that how the mixture pours is the first sign of quality. It should come out thick and lumpy and rich looking. Mine was perfecto. It oozed from the moist container and slowly slid to the bottom of the tall glass. Another sign of quality is how the shake is consumed. If you can suck it up a straw, it is much too thin. It you have to eat it with your spoon, it is just right. Again, this one was perfect. The final sign of quality is, of course, taste. The flavor must be rich and mellow and this one was exquisite with just a hint of vanilla.

I took a long time languishing over the milkshake. When I paid the bill, I praised the young waitress on her creation and told her the last milkshake I had here was over fifty years ago. She smiled politely, but didn't offer much in response. Departing the restaurant, it dawned on me the young lady was probably fifteen or sixteen and didn't exist fifty years ago, and for that matter, neither did her parents. But, for me, it was a lifetime.

Ralston's Drug Store Corner
(North and West Streets)

THE INN

Weeks before the first trip to Caldwell, I asked Pat Parks where I might stay. She suggested several options including The Inn at Belle Valley. I did not recognize the name until Pat explained it was the former Potts Motel on old Route 21 north of town. I then remembered taking pictures of the unit's construction for the newspaper, but I could not recall ever being inside, so staying there would be an adventure.

Pat told me the facility had recently been refurbished. I called The Inn and, being assured it was air conditioned, booked a room. The young lady I chatted with asked if I knew how to find The Inn. I told her I had lived in the area and knew exactly where it was. We exchanged pleasantries; I gave her my credit card information, and then from habit, asked for a confirmation number. She chuckled, and explained I only needed to present myself at the desk.

Arriving in Noble County after dark, I pulled off the interstate at Belle Valley and headed south on what is now labeled Ohio 821. Driving slowly along the two-lane road, I soon saw a neon sign marking The Inn's entrance. Turning into the gravel driveway, it seemed to me the front building was much prettier than I remembered.

The lobby was remarkable. It looked like a scene from the 1950s. A big old-fashioned red Coke cooler, with sliding top doors, prominently occupied part of the space. The other furnishings were similar in style and age. However, the young lady who appeared from a back room was quite contemporary. Smiling, she said, "You must be Wes Marshall."

We chatted about my visit as I filled out the booking card and I mentioned having taken photos of the original motel. She told me she and her husband were from northern Ohio and, while out on a casual drive, ended up in Noble County where they fell in love with the village. They bought the property and, over time, transformed it into The Inn, retaining its 1950s ambiance. She was excited to learn I had photos of the original buildings

My room was at the end of a unit back and above the office. Driving up, I had no idea what to expect, but like the lobby, the layout and fixtures were from the 1950s. I do not know how or where they got the furniture, but everything was immaculate and remarkably comfortable.

The room was longish and narrow with a dresser and luggage counter on the left and double beds on the right. In a back corner sat a table and two chairs next to the bathroom doorway. Placing suitcases on the counter, I wondered if the bathroom conversion would be as well done as the room itself. It was. Sparkling black and white tile and matching floor covering complemented bright shiny chrome fixtures.

Preparing for the trip, I had sorted through boxes of memorabilia to take along for the County Historical Society and friends. In that collection were pictures from my days with *The Journal* including one of the original motel. That photo I left with the Inn's owners.

Most mornings I was up early and could just hear the low rumble of nearby interstate traffic. Around me, fluffy morning mist drifted across surrounding hills and through the valleys. Occasionally, light pale sunbeams penetrated the mist to highlight leaves just starting to turn crimson and orange. Close by, a red barn trimmed in white sparkled in the morning light. The setting was as tranquil as a landscape painting until a jet thundered by high above on its way somewhere.

Before returning to Caldwell in 2003, I called The Inn only to find the phone out of service. Friends later told me the owners just disappeared, leaving the facility empty. Driving by, it saddened me to see weeds, an overgrown

lawn and an unlit neon sign. But, hopefully, someone else
will pick up the dream.

The Inn at Belle Valley (rear building)

GOOD EATS & GOOD FRIENDS

We rarely ate out when I was a kid. Going to Ogles restaurant below Dexter City was a special treat, and I can recall at least five restaurants around the Caldwell village square, although I am not sure they were all there at the same time. The one I remember most clearly was on West Street just north of the Roxy movie theater.

Like many eateries in other rural communities, it was called the *Home Restaurant,* or more commonly, just, "The Home." My compassion for meat loaf, mashed potatoes and brown gravy came from eating at the "Home." Like marshmallow milkshakes, good meat loaf with gravy is hard to find and something to cherish when found on a contemporary menu. The salty, rich taste of real brown gravy overflowing a volcano-like crater in fluffy mashed potatoes was the image I had in mind on my first Saturday night back in Caldwell.

Now, there are only a few restaurant choices around the village square and a few more near the interstate exit. I am not opposed to fast food, but I was in the mood for something not corporately formulated. Someone I had met mentioned Mom's restaurant south of town. The name seemed to promise what I was looking for and "Mom" was about as close to "Home" as I was likely to find.

Pulling off the road, I parked at a smallish, single story structure that appeared homey and a bit worn. A half-dozen cars were parked in the lot and, inside, folks were having dinner around several tables. The aroma of cooking food spilled from a rear kitchen and immediately tweaked my saliva glands. An older woman, presumably "Mom," cooked while two young girls, presumably daughters, waited table. But I did not verify relationships and my presumptions are not always accurate.

The menu was engaging for two reasons. To my dismay, it did not include meat loaf, but it did offer a roast beef sandwich with mashed potatoes and gravy that was close enough. But I looked twice at the meal prices. The entrée with salad, rolls and a bottomless drink was less than seven dollars. I have eaten in restaurants where a bottle of water cost that much!

One young lady took my order and disappeared into the kitchen. Waiting for the meal, I glanced around and saw several faces that seemed familiar. The, *seems familiar,* thought was a constant, and sometimes embarrassing, experience on both trips. Lots of friends looked mostly like they did years ago, only older. Others did not, and that was my dilemma at dinner. Did I, or did I not, know the couple several tables over?

They seemed to have the same problem because there were glances my way. Then the salad came, followed by the main dish and both were very good. Over coffee, I racked my brain trying to resurrect who they were. Finally, I connected images with names and realized it was Bob and Nancy Rudge. Nancy was in the high school band some of the time I was, and her husband was my optometrist through college.

Before I could move to the Rudge's table, the front door opened and in walked Francis Martin, with her daughter, Beth, and son-in-law Roger Sailing. Fran was the wife of Marvin Wood, our school band director for many years, and Beth was also in the band. Her husband, Roger, is a well-known local artist.

We all gathered for a nostalgic conversation packed with laughter and phrases like, "do you remember that," or "what fun it was to . . . ." Well into the discussion, I noticed Nancy's expression change. She looked like her mind was elsewhere. Then, her smile returned and, with a twinkle in her eye, she said, "Yes, Wes, they were great times, but I do hope you won't remember *everything!*" Clearly, an amusing and perhaps private recollection had come to her mind, but if it had anything to do with me, I have long since forgotten what it was.

I chose not to ask Nancy for clarification because I suspect it was a nice way for her to suggest some memories are best left untouched. That issue has haunted me throughout the writing of the book. My intrusion into lives and memories was never intended to be too personal nor harmful in any way.

Driving back to Caldwell, I thought about dining at Mom's. It had been many, many years since I last walked into a restaurant and, by happenstance, encountered and enjoyed such good friends and food.

Across America, thousands of fast-food restaurants offer inexpensive and quick snacks frequently consumed in sell-imposed isolation. But, Mom's, and many others like it in rural settings, remain places for a leisurely meal often consumed in the fellowship of neighbors and close friends. What a marvelous way to dine.

OLIVE CEMETERY

Low dark clouds slowly drifted above, blending with light gray ground mist. The early morning moisture dripping about was somewhere between a heavy fog and a light drizzle. The road to the old Olive Cemetery was freshly paved. Its sharp black shape meandered upward, cresting in a grove of large pine trees. Black asphalt reflected the dim morning light. As I drove up the single lane track, I thought of my mother, father and stepmother buried above.

Topping the hill, I saw hundreds of graves floating in the mist in regimented geometric patterns. Burial sites marched over, down and around slopes like corn stalks on a hillside. Stopping the car beneath a large tree, I walked a few yards along a white gravel path. The lush deep green grass of an Appalachian fall morning spread around me. Birds flitted about, their calls muted by a steady moaning whisper of a wind. All about me I felt near silence as a deep sense of tranquility gently cloaked my mind.

Most of what I saw was monochromatic, but here and there splashes of color dotted the landscape. Drifting lazily down, golden yellow and bright orange fall leaves formed colorful ground quilts at the base of aging trees. In the distance, the muted colors of floral arrangements burned through a foggy mist that nearly obscured the graves they marked. Nearby, a vine and moss-covered mausoleum stood, its stained sandstone walls looking like an old Scottish castle discolored by the ages.

Motionless, I watched the mist begin to lighten and lift. As it rolled back off the hilltop, row upon row of stone markers seemed to float from the fog. Big and little gravestones took form and shape. And then the names became visible: Caldwell, Tilton, Pickenpaugh, Brown, Gray, Ford, Tarleton, Noble and many, many more. Some I knew, most I did not.

Awash in memories, I thought about what all these people accomplished over decades. Emotions of sadness and hope churned through me. Mystically, I could sense the spirits of the very young and the very old quietly resting in peace. Each, in his or her way, had brought joy to the village of my childhood.

Brilliant sun burned through the cloud cover as I walked north along one side of section seven, looking carefully at each gravestone. A bit off the gravel path I found markers for Mary Louse Marshall and Wesley B. Marshall and Jeannette K. Marshall.

Perhaps it was the warmth of the morning sun, or perhaps it was the caress of time, but I felt the presence of my father and mother deep within my heart. I would like to believe we met once again that day and, for just a moment, embraced in the love we shared. I will not join them in those Noble Hills, but my soul will be there forever.

COUNTY FAIR REVISITED

One reason to go back to Caldwell in late August, 2000 was to attend the Noble County Fair before writing on that topic. I thought walking the grounds, seeing the sites and smelling the smells would help refresh and sharpen my memory. It did all of that, but the visit also demonstrated how much things do change.

The Fairground is still where it was in the 1940s. Arriving at one gate, rental car air conditioning cranked to maximum, I powered down the window, purchased a ticket and cringed at the humid air rolling in from outside. Assuring me I would find a place to park, the attendant handed me a pass, pointed up hill and sent me on my way to yet another adventure.

A grassy area just below the crest of the hill offered ample parking spaces. Pulling into one, I could just see the top of the Ferris wheel slowly turning on the midway down to my left. With camera bag in hand, I opened the car's door and immediately heard the calliope-like sound of the

Merry-Go-Round and smelled the sharp odor of over-cooked hot dogs. *Great*, I thought, *just like I remembered!*

Five steps later, perspiration began dripping from my forehead as I mumbled to myself about Midwest humidity. Undaunted, I shuffled up the slope and arrived in the middle of the farm tractor display. Egad! These were all bright red and not the familiar green and yellow I expected. *Well,* I thought again, *maybe the John Deer display is somewhere else.* Then, looking north, I realized the animal barns were new and no longer the open ones I had lived in during band camp so many years before. But, to the south, the midway looked utterly familiar.

Rows of tented gaming stands formed a long narrow corridor with hawkers working the crowd and proclaiming a mere toss of the baseball or a hoop would win a valuable prize. *Yea, sure*, I thought, remembering the small fortune I had spent as a child trying to win a kewpie doll.

Most of the rides and concessions looked familiar and seemed to blur into a montage of color and motion, and all the smells were there: cotton candy, ice cones, home-made cherry pie and caramel corn. Excitedly, I began to snap pictures, carefully framing each shot through the camera's optical viewfinder.

Slowly, I panned from side to side seeking the perfect balance of form and content. The focus button shifted everything from fuzzy to crisp, and the next image to come into focus nearly caused me to drop the camera.

There, in the precise center of my viewfinder was a *burrito stand* with a red, white and green sign promoting authentic Mexican food.

Stunned, I lowered the camera and just stared at the colorful little trailer. Never, in my wildest dreams had I expected to see such a sight at the Noble County Fair. When I grew up in Caldwell, Mexican food was virtually unknown to us and pizza was yet to come. Living in the Southwest has caused me to become nearly as fond of cheese enchiladas as meat loaf, but tacos and burros in Noble County struck me as amusingly incongruous, indeed un-American. Then, reality set in, and I understood it was very *American,* because whatever works – works.

Obviously, times have changed. Had I looked harder, I might have stumbled onto a Chinese fast food stand amidst all the other food places or maybe Emeril Lagasse cooking Cajun. I suppose the Mexican food was probably just fine, but it will not be part of the memories I take home. I plan to dream about homemade hamburgers, fresh country corn dripping in butter and gritty with salt, and a big old glass of ice-cold apple cider.

Noble County Fair, 2000

ALONG THE THREE FORKS ROAD

Harley Fowler and I went to school together. I fondly remember his black Model-A Ford and frequently pushing it to the Standard Oil station for gas. He worked at that station when he was in school and the owner gave him some paint to redo the Ford because the original black was slowly rusting away. The finished paint job was very nice and it was probably the only Model-A ever to be adorned with bright blue Standard Oil paint.

Harley and I graduated in 1953 and went our separate ways. He eventually ended up in Phoenix and we saw each other maybe once or twice during the many years we both lived in Arizona. We met again at a Caldwell High School reunion in June of 1999. There wasn't much time to chat then, but I learned he had moved back to Noble County and was living on the old Woodford farm where his wife grew up. His decision to return to the area intrigued me. I wondered what it would be like to return to one's roots after so many years away. So, I set out to find the farm along a narrow winding lane south of Caldwell.

The road to Three Forks rambles up through a gorgeous, tree lined little valley with modest homes every thousand yards or so on each side. I had an address, but mail box numbers are small and my eyesight was never especially good. If I can read the name on a mailbox, I've probably run into it. My search, therefore, was slow and frustrating.

Several trips up and down the valley were unsuccessful. I thought surely someone along the road would know everyone else, and all I needed to do was stop and ask where my friend lived. Ahead, I saw a chap working by a new barn on the right side of the road. I turned onto a short gravel driveway, rolled down the window and realized the person walking toward me was Harley.

Well, we had a terrific visit. I learned he had retired in Phoenix but eventually became uncomfortable with the large metropolitan area. He said he had always yearned for the quiet simple life of his youth. That desire eventually took him back to Noble County. He and his wife fixed up the old farmhouse, added a big barn and seemed to be having a ball.

Wanda brought us cool drinks from their house and joined us for a few minutes. It was a warm summer afternoon and we welcomed the cool refreshment. She listened to us chat for a while and then asked Harley to back the ATV out of the barn for her. It was parked tight along side a tractor and SUV. He did, and she bounced off across country to gather fresh beans in the nearby woods.

Harley motioned me to follow him, and we ambled down toward a small stream slightly below the barn. There he talked of a recent flood that raged through the area and damaged the channel. The event motivated him to get out his tractor and, as he put it, "Straighten it all up a bit." We came to a lovely grassy tree-shaded area along the stream. Scattered here and there were places to sit and relax or read. The seats were carved out of tree stumps or made from parts of an old tractor. He gestured up the hillside and said he had other little places like this where he could just rest awhile and enjoy the peace and quiet.

I asked him what he did to occupy his time. Wiping his face with a red bandanna he thought about how to answer my question. "Well," he said. "I get up on good mornings and I move a little dirt over here." Then, pointing in another direction with a twinkle in his eye, he continued, "then I decide to put it over there."

In a more serious tone, he spoke of helping neighbors dig foundations, improve driveways or clear fields. And all through the conversation he waved at folks driving by on the nearby road, identifying each person by name, family history and what they did now. Some, he noted, were going home and others were headed up into the hills to feed their horses or cattle.

Our chat wound down as the sun started to set. The upper end of the valley began to darken in deep purple shadows. Harley said his health was good, and he felt the best he ever had. He looked around and then back at me. "Helping folks," he said, "is kind of a pay back for all the good things Wanda and I enjoy here."

We exchanged addresses, shook hands and bid farewell as he walked me to the car. I got in and looked back at Harley through the side window. His eyes were focused up the valley toward a far ridge. Then his gaze shifted back to me as he said, "It's great to be here." The message I heard was *I'm back home now.*

KNOWING YOUR VINO

During the first trip back to Noble County, I asked my cousin, Tally Hill, and an old friend, Fran Martin, to join me for dinner to reminisce about the Caldwell High School band. Caldwell is in Olive Township, an area where alcohol is not sold, and I wanted to have a glass of wine with dinner. At their suggestion, we headed north to Cambridge and a restaurant not far off the interstate.

Going north by Belle Valley triggered memories of the Golden Plaza and the Oasis. Both bars are still there. As a very young child I recall riding to Belle Valley with my parents. Later, as a teenager, I would make the trip to Belle Valley by myself or with friends.

The beverage choices I remember back then were beer, whiskey and hard cider. I know wine must have been available, but my peers and I knew little about it. In fact, I suspect we probably thought wine was something women drank and men did not. Much later in life I would acquire a taste for wine and, eventually, the knowledge to select it with some consistency.

Fran identified our destination on the outskirts of Cambridge. We exited the freeway and drove toward a cluster of buildings topped with the green neon sign of a national hotel chain. Pulling into a parking space, I imagined the bouquet and color of a deep rich red cabernet.

A smiling young waitress led us to a nicely decorated window table and left us alone as we chatted and looked through the menu. The wine list was modest. There was a common national brand and "house" selections. Reds and whites were listed under both categories, but, as is common, the house wines were less expensive. Experience has taught me price is not always the best measure of wine.

In time, I asked the waitress what the difference was between the two wine lists, my intention being to find out who made the house wines. A bit flustered, she disappeared into a back area and then returned. Pointing to the menu, she explained, "Well, these are the Woodbridge wines and those are the house wines." When I asked for a glass of red wine, she hesitantly recommended a chardonnay.

Frustrated, I almost lost my cool, and then it dawned on me I was the problem, not the young waitress. It was not her fault she was unfamiliar with wine. Clearly, beer and liquor remain the area's beverages of choice, and time has not changed the preferences I grew up with; I have changed.

The food was good, the conversation wonderful. We shared memories of 1950s band life well into dessert. And, for the record, the first glass of house cabernet was not bad. The second one was much better.

DEPARTING

The morning was cool and mostly clear. I had arranged to meet Al and Linda Christopher for breakfast in Zanesville on the way to Columbus and my flight back to Tucson. Linda and I have kept in touch since high school and I had joined them for dinner at the beginning of my visit in 2000.

Driving north to Belle Valley, I witnessed a September morning sun slowly rise over the eastern hills, its pale light glaring off small tranquil farm ponds tucked here and there in the green hillsides. Brush strokes of fluffy clouds stood out in stark contrast to a deep blue morning sky.

Turning onto I-77, the twin concrete ribbons seemed to disappear into the distance in diminishing perspective. Familiar signs flashed by: Wolf Run, Pleasant City, Senecaville, Byesville and then Cambridge. Huge semi-trucks rumbled in the opposite direction. Tall cellular phone towers dotted the rolling hillsides, each one reminding me it was the 21st century.

Turning onto I-70 and then west to Zanesville, I thought back over the previous four days and all the people I had met and talked with. Some were new, but most were old friends who shared my life many years ago. As folks are fond of saying, people of my age are approaching the twilight of life. Memories fade as aches and pains grow. Eyes dim and bodies bend under the weight of life. Yet, every person I talked with spoke joyously of the good times, both past and present.

In 2003, I had a grand time meeting old classmates at my 50th high school reunion in May and meeting many other friends at an all-school gathering in June. My wife, Marilyn, joined me for part of the second trip. We enjoyed a post reunion gathering at the Barnharts' and a delightful Sunday morning breakfast at the Ralstons' and then headed south towards Athens and, for me, a nostalgic tour of the Ohio University campus.

Both departures were emotional, but without sorrow. The days were beautiful, the hills brilliant green, and I was at peace with the world. We chatted about my meeting a chap who had migrated to the States from Portsmouth, England and now lived on a ridge south of Caldwell with a beautiful view of the village. It was fascinating to realize two people from such diverse

NOBLE HILLS

backgrounds could share the same love and fondness for the same area.

The previous fall, Marilyn and I had toured southern England and ironically, as it turned out, stayed in a small bed and breakfast on Spice Island in Portsmouth near where the man had grown up. Now, he lives where I grew up and each day enjoys the peaceful and ever changing beauty of the valley below and the people who live there.

It is indeed a small world, and more than ever, I understand that regardless of where I am, or where I live, a small part of me will always remain deep within the Noble Hills. In an odd sort of way, one can never really *go back* home because one never *totally leaves* home.

fixx

NOBLE HILLS

THANKS

My, where does one begin? Literally all the people I have ever known in Caldwell and Noble County made this book possible. Were it not for those relationships, and many lingering friendships, these stories and essays would not be documented, nor have true meaning. But there are some people who have been especially helpful.

Tally Hill, my cousin and eldest child of my mother's oldest brother, shared memories with me as did Dorothy Hill, wife of my mother's youngest brother. Their recollections and comments were most helpful.

Pat Parks was a constant source of encouragement and insight. Her historic articles in *The Journal* provided background for some of the stories. Bud and Bev Ralston read early versions of the book and offered support and ideas.

Over many years of loyal friendship, Linda and Al Christopher helped keep me in touch with Noble County as did Julia (McGregor) Thornberry.

Portions of the book (Part I) were printed in *The Journal* in serial form and my thanks to David Evans, Sally Delancy and the staff for doing so and coping with writings that did not easily fit the paper's format. The material prompted over fifty letters, notes and E-mail messages from across America. My sincere thanks to each of those readers and to the three who graciously agreed to share their comments and are quoted on the back cover.

During the last trip back, I had a chance to meet and chat with Roger Pickenpaugh, a quite successful local author. He gave me several of his books and offered helpful publishing advice.

Dr. Peggy Dunlap, a dear Tucson friend, volunteered to edit the material before final printing and she did a wonderful job. However, some errors are inevitable, and the ones you find are mine, not Peggy's.

The sketches scattered throughout the book are digitally generated from photographs I took over several years. There are two exceptions: the aerial view of the Village of Caldwell and the photo of Samuel Caldwell. Both of these came from a publication of *The Journal* titled "Caldwell Municipal Building," (Dedicated Saturday, July 13, 1957}. I clearly recall helping to put that document together, but the photographer is not identified.

I do wish to extend a very special thanks to my wife, Marilyn. She has been a constant source of encouragement, and a willing listener. We have lost count of the number of times she patiently listened to me read portions of the book. Although not raised in Noble County, she shares my love and compassion for rural Ohio and the thousands and thousands of small villages like Caldwell that continue to thrive throughout America.

Finally, a brief comment on the subjects of sentimentality and motivation, perhaps best illustrated by recreating a conversation I had with a friend who had just read portions of the book. It went something like this:

"Are you sure you grew up in the same place I did? I don't remember doing all that stuff." My friend challenged.

"Well, some of it I remembered and some of it was what I thought probably happened."

"Isn't making stuff up in a history book sort of cheating?"

"Actually," I replied, "It's not a history book. It's a collection of memories."

My friend considered the answer for a bit and then continued his observations. "You know you don't talk much about bad memories."

"No, I don't . . . just the good ones."

"Why did you do that?"

"The happy times are more fun, and one nice thing about writing is you can write about what you want and forget about what you don't want."

"Well frankly," he commented," a lot of the stories are sort of mushy and do-goody."

"Yes, I guess they are, but I would use a different way of describing them."

"OK, so why do you get so worked up about little old Caldwell?"

"Isn't everyone?"

"You're kidding," He replied.

"Nope, I think a lot of folks feel the same way about their hometown, big or small."

"Ahhh, you're crazy."

"Yea, probably, but I'd say *sentimental.* That's what I am, and always hope to be. I get warm and fuzzy thinking about growing up in Caldwell. Those who don't share those emotions have somehow missed a wonderful sense of heritage and belonging . . . or maybe they just lost it somewhere along the way."

Smiling, my friend chuckled, "Hey, that's pretty heavy stuff. "Did you write the book because you're sentimental?"

"Partly," I answered. "But it's more than that. I believe it's important to share some of our wonderful childhood experiences with younger generations, especially my grandchildren. We can never go back to those quieter times, but learning how life was back then might help others find a better life today."

"You're getting philosophical."

238

"Yea, I suppose so. But I am what I am -- molded and nurtured in the hills of the Allegheny Plateau in a little county called Noble -- and that's the way it is."